ONE FOOT IN A SPANISH GRAVE

ONE FOOT IN A SPANISH GRAVE

Translated by MÍCHEÁL Ó HAODHA

edited and introduced by BARRY MCLOUGHLIN

Maps by ANDRÉ NOVAK

with a contribution from his nephew BRENDAN BYRNE

UNIVERSITY COLLEGE DUBLIN PRESS
PREAS CHOLÁISTE OLLSCOILE BHAILE ÁTHA CLIATH
2023

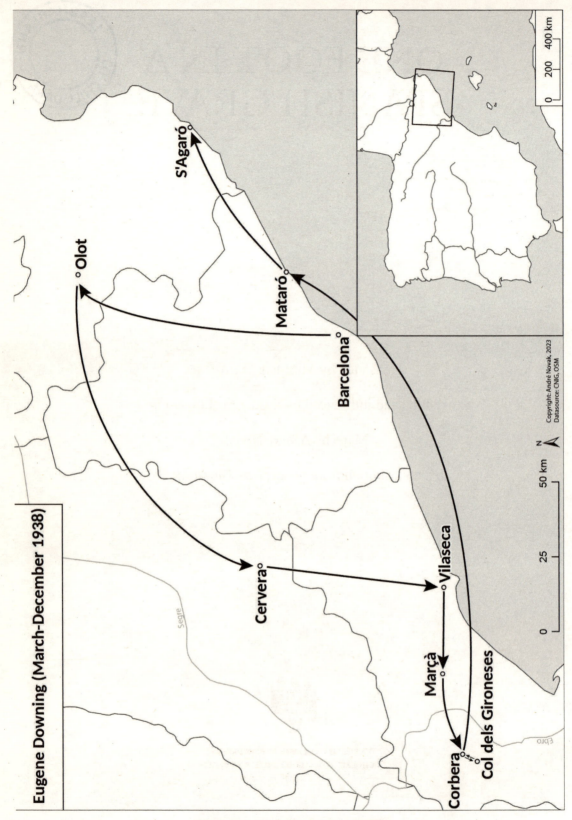

Eugene Downing's military postings, April to December 1938

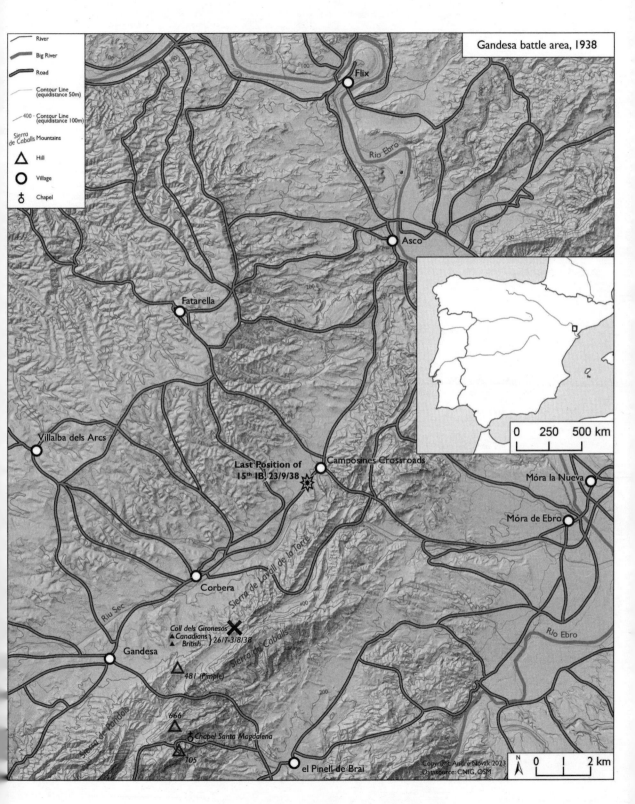

Legend

- River
- Big River
- Road
- Contour Line (equidistance 50m)
- 400 — Contour Line (equidistance 100m)

Sierra de Caballs Mountains

- △ Hill
- ⬡ Village
- ⛪ Chapel

Gandesa battle area, 1938

Flix

Asco

Fatarella

Villalba dels Arcs

Last Position of 15th IB, 23/9/38

Camposines Crossroads

Móra la Nueva

Móra de Ebro

Rio Ebro

Corbera

Sierra de la vall de la Torre

Coll dels Gironesos
▲ *Canadians* ✕ 26/7–3/8/38
▲ *British*

Sierra del Caballs

Gandesa

△ *481 (Pimple)*

Riu Sec

△ *666*

⛪ *Chapel Santa Magdalena*

△ *705*

el Pinell de Brai

Sierra de Pandols

Copyright Andre Novak 2023
Datasource: CNIG, OSM

0   250   500 km

N
0   1   2 km

Ebro battle, Gandesa valley. X marks where Eugene Downing was wounded, 26 July 1938

First published 2023
by University College Dublin Press
UCD Humanities Institute, Room H103,
Belfield,
Dublin 4

www.ucdpress.ie

Text and notes © the editors, 2023

ISBN 978-19-1-08207-66

This text is a translation of Eoghan Ó Duinnín's (Eugene Downing's) book *La Niña Bonita agus An Róisín Dubh: Cuimhní Cinn ar Chogadh Cathartha na Spáinne* (An Clóchomhar, Baile Átha Cliath, 1986).

The Irish-language rights for this book lie with Cló Iar-Chonnacht, Indreabhán, Co. na Gaillimhe.

CIP data available from the British Library

Typeset in Dublin by Gough Typesetting Limited
Text design by Lyn Davies
Printed in Scotland on acid-free paper by [?????]

A Dedication for Brendan Byrne

My father Brendan passed away in March 2023, after a long illness. It meant a great deal to him to know that this translation of Eugene's book would shortly be published, and we talked about it often in his last few weeks. Dad was so proud of Eugene's life and legacy, and proud too of having protected and preserved his writing and records for so many years and representing Eugene at International Brigade commemorations and events.

Eugene's influence on my Dad was evident, from their shared love of history – particularly texts that recorded the lives and words of real people, above revered academic works; their lifelong commitment to socialism, democracy, and the labour movement; and, of course, their passion for books, preferably stacked floor to ceiling. And Eugene took great pride in my Dad too, going so far as to tell us that our father was an intellectual. Dad, being a humbler man, found this praise very embarrassing.

Dad loved and respected Eugene so much, and always wanted a wider audience to be able to read his story. That will include many members of Eugene's family – despite Eugene's encouragement, and eventual exasperation, none of us were good enough at Irish to be able to read *La Niña Bonita agus an Róisín Dubh* in its original publication. But as both my Mum and Dad made sure that Uncle Eugene was a big part of our childhood, on the many Sundays he spent at our house we were lucky enough to hear his stories straight from the horse's mouth… not that Eugene would be thrilled with that analogy. I can imagine the rueful face he would make, the 'tsk, tsk' and slow shake of his head at my use of such a cliché. Or perhaps he'd make one of his darkly funny comments along the lines of three-legged horses being of no use to anyone. Then he would laugh and knock on his artificial leg, something that never failed to delight and shock us.

We were fascinated, of course, by the story of how Eugene lost his leg. And by the stories of the young Irish men and women who had travelled in secret to Spain, to help in the fight against Franco. Long before we were taught the basic outlines of World War II in school, we knew about the danger of fascism and how it must be opposed, even though the cost can be terrible, and victory is not assured. As a child, I really struggled to understand that – there was another war in Europe that Fascists won? I asked my Dad endless 'but why?' questions about it. Had Eugene lost his leg for nothing? Nine-year-olds can be very Manichean in their outlook.

Dad patiently tried to explain the complexity and cruelty and compromise of the Spanish Civil War to me. They lost, he said, but it was not for nothing. There is right and there is wrong. Sometimes it's easy to tell which is which. Sometimes it's not. For the volunteers of the International Brigade, like Eugene, it was very clear.

But how did they know, I asked him.

They could see the truth of what was happening, Dad said. From reading newspapers and books and letters, from hearing the stories of the people who were there. From the evidence and from the witnesses. That's how.

My great-uncle was a witness. He told his story in his native Irish, almost 50 years after his return from the Ebro. My wonderful Dad made sure that story was safeguarded for another four decades after that. And now in this new translated edition, this story, this important testimony, will be shared once again. I hope it reaches many new readers.

The Byrne and Downing family is incredibly proud of these two remarkable men, Eugene Downing and Brendan Byrne, and so grateful to everyone who has worked so painstakingly on this publication.

No pasarân.

Elizabeth Byrne
May 2023

Contents

Translator's Note

This text is a translation of Eoghan Ó Duinnín's (Eugene Downing's) book *La Niña Bonita agus An Róisín Dubh: Cuimhní Cinn ar Chogadh Cathartha na Spáinne* (An Clóchomhar, Baile Átha Cliath, 1986).

The translation is an amended version of the original Irish Ms.: the English text follows a chronological order, part of the original introductory texts have been omitted, and foot notes have been added to those of Eugene Downing (ED) by me (MÓH) and Barry McLoughlin (BM). Barry thankfully edited the English text, added the index and suggested changes.

We have not amended Downing's statements in accordance with the tenets of political correctness.

Eugene was a man of his time, and we are grateful to have been bequeathed this important historical record of his, particularly given the fact that so few of his peers or those of similar political affiliation chose to write about their lives.

Summarised biographical details of the Irish volunteers fighting for Republican Spain can be found in:

Barry McLoughlin & Emmet O'Connor, *In Spanish Trenches: The Minds and Deeds of the Irish who Fought for the Republic in the Spanish Civil War* (UCD Press, 2020)

Barry McLoughlin, *Fighting for Republican Spain: Frank Ryan and the Volunteers from Limerick in the International Brigades* (Lulu Books, 2014)

https://www.mcloughlin.at/wp-content/uploads/2020/09/Biographies-Irish-IB.pdf – E

Mícheál Ó hAodha
Gaillimh, March 2023

Remembering Eugene Downing

My first memory of my Uncle Eugene's presence in our lives was the huge 500cc Norton motorbike parked in the hallway of our grandparents' house in Neagh Road where we then lived with my parents. This was Eugene's, bought on his return from London in 1946. My parents and grandparents had moved into the newly built Mount Tallant Scheme in 1938. My grandparents and sons Seán and Eugene left no 2 Cuffe Street which was part of the tenement buildings being demolished for a mixture of road widening and to make room for the construction of new flats.

My parents moved in at that time to make up the numbers, in order to coincide with the then Dublin Corporation allocation criteria, big families getting preference. Eugene was then over in Spain and only spent two or three weeks in Neagh Road after his return in December 1938, then moving to London within a month and staying there for the duration of the war. Seán also departed from Terenure in 1942 to seek employment in London where he was to remain for the rest of his life.

This huge 500cc Norton was later replaced by a small boxy Ford car. That motor bike, a house full of books and a piano will always feature in my early recollections of Eugene. We had a large piano bought by my father, a rather grand affair which was parked in the small front parlour and on which Eugene would from time to time bang out some tune. 'Another string to his bow', as he taught himself to read music and hammered away.

That and the books were part of Eugene's stock. When he returned from London, he initially worked with Tom O'Brien from a premises in Parliament Street. O'Brien who was also an ex-International Brigader who had served on the Ebro Front and had founded a small typing duplicating service with Eleanor O'Brien (no relation), including a small lending library.

There was a parting of the ways and Eugene branched out on his own, establishing a small travelling library *The Regular Library*. He rented out books travelling door to door, building up a large customer base. Most rooms in our house including the attic were shelved and overflowed with books – romances, westerns, thrillers, detective stories (I can still recall the yellow-covered hardbacks *Bloodhound Detective*, with the trademark bloodhound with the deerstalker hat on the spine).

Eugene bought his stock in bulk from various sources in the book dealers' trade, *Banba Books* being one. Our family had of course moved out in 1948 to our own house in Inchicore but we were regular visitors to our grandparent also, us children being required to spend holidays at Easter and Christmas to keep them company.

I recall sleeping in the small back room I shared with Eugene, who then smoked roll ups incessantly and never seemed to sleep, the light from his cigarette glowing in the dark. The *Regular Library* flourished for a time. Eugene used to rent out the books for 4 pence per week, and jokingly boasted that he had an amazing return on capital invested: 'Buy a Western for 1 shilling, and if I lend it out 60 times that 240 pence equals 20 shillings, versus initial cost of 1 shilling. Sure, you wouldn't get that on the stock exchange.'

This was in an era before mass market paperbacks and provided a steady regular income. Eugene also diverted into other ventures. He once rented a shop in Dalkey on a five-year lease and opened a secondhand bookshop. I was drafted in to publicise it with a leaflet drop in the district: *BOOKS BOOKS BOOKS BOOKS TO SUIT ALL TASTES*. He initially opened the shop Tuesday and Thursday evenings and all day Saturday, on which day I was deputised to attend.

This venture may have been before its time in Dalkey. I recall one dreary Saturday when I had one solitary customer who bought a magazine because it had a picture of Grace Kelly on the cover. This couldn't last and Eugene took issue with the landlord, claiming he had been misled as to the footfall on the street (the only foot fall being his own), so he went on rent strike, stopped paying rent and slowly de-stocked the shop. Finally, on one particular evening, we loaded up Eugene's car to the roof with the remaining stock, dismantled the shelving, dropped the key into the landlord's letterbox and vamoosed into the hills.

'Now let him sue me if he likes', being Eugene's farewell comment. Things rested so. Socially he was a regular visitor to the home of Seán Redmond and his family, who then lived in Dublin. We referred to him as 'old Seán' to distinguish him from 'young Seán', later active in the Connolly Association when the family moved to London When you are close to somebody you are never aware of the effect he has on other people. Tom Redmond told me at his funeral that Eugene's weekly visits to the Redmond household in both Dublin and later in London were always welcomed:

> Eugene taught me how to play chess and there was great excitement when we knew he was coming over to visit. He was a dutiful and respectful son, his strong anti-clerical views didn't inhibit him from driving his mother down to Mass in Mount Argus every Sunday and waiting for her in the back pew until Mass was completed.'

As regards his active political life, his hands-on involvement may have diminished, but not his strong left-wing opinions. While he did do some work for the Communist Party, driving for Mick O'Riordan in a General Election in the 1950s (*The Catholic Standard* reaching new heights by extolling the faithful with red-inked posters DON'T VOTE FOR THE RED O'RIORDAN), his allegiance to the Communist Party of Ireland (CPI) as such waned somewhat.

He recalled once meeting Young Jim Larkin, then a Labour Party TD, in Molesworth Street. Young Jim was a former graduate of the Lenin School in Moscow who had drifted away from the CPI, never formally leaving it. Eugene asked him why he had dropped out of the Party. Larkin explained that he had often had long political and economic discussions with Johnny Nolan, then a veteran Party stalwart, and Nolan would come up with clear logical answers which seemed to clarify the issues. But the problem was, as Larkin explained 'the system doesn't work and if it doesn't work, there is something wrong with it, and I don't have to know what's wrong with it.'

I recall that I was once avidly saving clippings from the newspapers dealing with the Hungarian Uprising that dominated the news in late 1956. Eugene told me I was wasting my time: 'The story you should be concentrating on is Suez, that's more significant.'

Christmas time was Abbey Pantomime time and Eugene usually treated both my brother Gerard and me to tickets to the performances then staged in the Queen's Theatre. Two particular performances stick out in my recollection: *Brian agus an Claidheamh Solus* and *Ulysses agus Penelope* with a blond, bewigged Ray McNally in the starring role.

Eugene continued with the traveling library up to late 1960, and at this stage moved to live with our family in Rathfarnham, where he coexisted peacefully enough with my father and mother despite my father's uneasiness when Eugene occasionally held forth for our amusement and astonishment: hair-raising stories about the Medieval Popes and their numerous mistresses and progeny.

The book rental business began to falter with the growth in the paperback market and Eugene for a time *diverted* into providing a typing/duplication service, also spending some time compiling printing and publishing an Irish/English glossary for enthusiastic GAA fans: *Páirc na Imeartha*. It included phrases such as: 'Well played, lads' and 'Good shot' or 'Great goal'. It didn't include an Irish translation for *'The referee's a wa—ker'*, GAA fans of that era being of a more refined disposition.

However, the pressing need to earn a steadier and more regular income prompted Eugene to depart once again for London in early 1961. In his second stint working in London, he had a variety of jobs, primarily clerical, including one with United Artists, and latterly with the London Gas Board. His social life revolved around membership of the Gaelic League and the Irish Club, and weekly visits to his brother Seán, his wife Joyce and children, in Hornsey. There he enjoyed the companionship of his three nieces who remember him with affection and recall his enthusiasm and interest in their activities. He was faddish about food, and deciding that lentils were particularly healthy, insisted, when visiting his brother, that lentil soup be on the menu, bringing along packets of lentils. He encouraged Joyce to make soup every time, until the family got fed up with drinking lentil soup at every meal. In addition, he resumed his friendship with Seán Redmond and his wife, and mingled socially with the Redmond family in their London home in Tufnell Park.

He came home to Ireland regularly with stopovers in Dublin en route to the Gaeltacht. His arrival was always greeted with excitement. His presence was very stimulating. Eugene retired to Dublin to live permanently there, initially in Ranelagh, and eventually he moved to live with his niece Gabrielle and her family in Valleymount, County Wicklow, again enjoying the company and sharing in the lives, times and tribulations of his many grandnieces and grandnephews until his death in his ninetieth year on 24 July 2003.

Brendan Byrne
March 2021

The Irish in the International Brigades: An Introduction

by Barry McLoughlin

Of the 250 Irish-born volunteers who served in the International Brigades (IB) during the Spanish Civil War Eugene Downing (Eoghan Ó Duinnín) was a member of the last batch to be recruited in Ireland. The first group, chosen by Frank Ryan, left Dublin for Spain in December 1936. Since the losses among these early arrivals were heavy (seven were killed in the Battle of Lopera after Christmas 1936), Frank Ryan, probably in consultations with Seán Murray, leader of the Irish Communist Party, and Peadar O'Donnell and others on the Republican Left, discouraged further recruitment within the Irish Free State. This self-imposed veto was lifted in early spring 1938, when Murray sanctioned the sending of seven party members, who joined four veterans returning to the battlefield on their long journey through England and France before the strenuous climb over the Pyrenees.

Over sixty left from Ireland, over double that number from Britain, only twelve from the US, thirty from Canada and three from Australia. Only three Irish counties (Westmeath, Roscommon, Wicklow) are missing from the brigaders' county of origin, with Dublin and Belfast dominating and sizeable contingents from the Northern counties, Waterford, and Cork. The greatest influx of Irishmen into Albacete (the main base of the International Brigades) was recorded for late 1936/early 1937 and included a few doubtful characters. Those who came later were, arguably, more reliable and properly vetted when the brigades became more organised as a military force. Irish fatalities in Spain were much higher than World War One averages, 72 dead at 29 per cent. Conditions of service were exceedingly hard: bad equipment, shoddy uniforms, inadequate rations, and the lack of proper medical treatment which resulted in unnecessary deaths, 'last resort' amputations and operations without the prerequisite anesthetics. As the People's Army of the Spanish Republic lacked trained commissioned officers and NCOs and promotions within the International Brigades often owed more to a 'good Party record' than military prowess, leadership in the field was often disastrously amateurish and wasteful of life.

The proportion of communists among the Irish is relatively low at about half, as compared to about 60 per cent in the brigades as a whole. At least one third of the Irish had a republican record (IRA, Republican Congress) and a handful had fought in the War of Independence and the Civil War. Up to 30 had served in the Irish Free State Army or British Army, while a handful comprised Western Front veterans. The average age of the Irish IB volunteers was high for a modern war – 26. Little is known about many Irishmen recruited in Britain, while the strong Irish section in the Canadian battalion were almost all communists.

One is cautious in making any other generalisations about the Irish on the side of the Spanish Republic, save to admire the bravery of most and admit the obvious: that a sizeable Irish minority (as in the English, Welsh, and Scottish contingents) who were unsuitable for military life, undisciplined, prone to drunkenness and resented their lot so much that some deserted. In a 'normal' army, stints in the 'glasshouse' would have deterred bad behaviour, but discipline in the brigades was supposed to be self-imposed because of the common anti-fascist commitment. Of the 40 Irish that went AWOL, about a third served a stretch on punishment duties before reintegration and at least 24 managed to leave the country illegally, usually on a British ship. Notorious troublemakers were expelled from Spain; others were permitted to leave on age and psychiatric grounds. Under-age or unsuitable recruits who had slipped through the vetting process in London, were regularly rejected in Paris (medical examination) or after interviews in Figueras (the assembly point in Catalonia). In the second half of 1937, after the Battle of Brunete (July 1937), there were a considerable number of Irish repatriation cases, usually men who had been wounded in battle or those supported by their leader Frank Ryan, who, fearing further heavy casualties, thought they 'had done enough'.

The quality of the military training for English-speakers improved over time, due in part to the establishment of a base, entailing at least three months' education, in Tarazona de la Mancha in the summer of 1937. In the early battles around Madrid, where the first Irish fatalities were recorded (Tommy Patten, Bill 'Blue' Barry), there was no weapon instruction beforehand, their use was imparted in the desperate combat at close quarters in the buildings of the new university or in the villages on the city's outskirts.[1] The first major battle in which English-speakers (XV IB) were involved was to save the Madrid-Valencia road to the south-east after Franco's forces had crossed the Jarama river from the west and were scaling the heights on the other side. Many of the British and Irish thrown against them in mid-February 1937 had never fired a shot in anger as their scanty training with unloaded weapons had been curtailed when the front broke. They held the line, as did some Irish serving in the American battalion, but at enormous cost: 16 dead and countless wounded. Their next encounter with the enemy was planned to be the first victory of Republican forces in which all IB units were involved. But the Battle of Brunete in the torrid July heat did not smash the fascist salient west of the capital, gaining only a few ruined villages before the carnage subsided after three weeks because both sides were exhausted. At least nine Irishmen were killed. The list of the wounded was long and the XV IB lost over three quarters of its strength. Morale was now at a low ebb in the British Battalion and remained so even after some memorable victories (Quinto, Belchite) during the Aragon campaign shortly afterwards. With the arrival of new recruits and increased combat efficacy the English-speakers acquitted themselves well amid the snows of Teruel at the turn of the year, but disaster was to strike in the early spring.

The Internationals were swept aside during March 1938 in a huge onslaught of Francoist and Italian troops in Aragon that reached the sea in the east and cut the Republic in two. The 'March Retreats' were an unmitigated disaster: hundreds were killed outright, shot out of hand, went missing, deserted, or were taken prisoner in large numbers after the bridges over the fast-flowing Ebro had been dynamited. At Calaceite, on 31 March, the British Battalion ran into Italian mobile columns. Over 150 were killed or wounded and 140 taken prisoner, including Frank Ryan and over 20 of his countrymen. For many of them it was their first day in battle for they had been mobilised at short notice at their barracks in Tarazona and sent in battalion strength to stem the tide. What followed was the slow re-building of units and morale, with many new recruits from Britain and Ireland, in what proved to be the longest stretch from front-line duty during the entire war. For nearly three months the volunteers rested and trained in villages in southern Catalonia, and the general mood improved despite severe shortages of food and equipment. This is where Eugene Downing enters the picture, an enthusiastic novice willing to learn the craft of warfare under the strict eye of his commander, Lieutenant Paddy O'Sullivan.

So morale was high when the Internationals crossed the Ebro in late July, entering territory they had been driven from four months previously. In the words of the English historian Richard Baxell, it was 'the last throw of the dice'[2], a desperate effort to prolong the struggle until the major war most expected would break out between the democracies and Hitler during the 'Sudeten Crisis'. The capitulation to Hitler at Munich shattered that hope, and its timing coincided with the final destruction of the brigades just before they were to be withdrawn and repatriated. The Battle of Ebro started well for the volunteers from Ireland and Britain in a concerted drive towards the important town of Gandesa. Badly equipped, without sufficient artillery or air-cover, the battalions were bled white while fighting in attempts to gain the heights south of the town. The end came when they were being driven back towards the river: on the last day of combat, 23 September, the British battalion was routed. Company commander Jack Nalty and company commissar Bill McGregor were killed in that last encounter, bringing the Irish fatality toll in the Ebro campaign to 13. The survivors were repatriated in December, as were the prisoners-of-war, released in groups after being exchanged for Italians.

Memoirs of IB veterans from Ireland are rare, and those who did write were committed socialists or communists. One of the merits of Eugene Downing's account is that it presents the reader with a view from a 'rank and file' committed volunteer eager to be seen as a good soldier. However, Eugene, with his wry view of the world shared by comrades such as Michael Lehane, disliked political proselytizers and overbearing or insensitive political commissars, excoriated as 'comic stars' by not a few Americans. Downing went to Spain to fight not to be preached at, and the primacy of military efficiency he shared was strictly adhered to by his countrymen who had important posts in the British Battalion, especially Paddy O'Sullivan, Jack Nalty and Paddy O'Daire. In the final phase of the war, the Irish held positions in the four companies of the British battalion out of proportion to their numbers (27 in the battalion total of 558): two company commanders (Nalty and O'Daire) and two company commissars (Johnny Power and Bill McGregor). Absent in his memoir are any mentions of deep personal feelings about losing his left leg below the knee – he was wounded in the second day of the Ebro battle – or whether he had post-traumatic mental problems. His generation, including those who served through World War Two, were disinclined to talk about the terror and pity of warfare or its long-term effects. Humorous stories about the inanities of military life were the only aspects of soldiering likely to be imparted to the curious and well-meaning listener. One surmised that it was in keeping with his character: most Irish of his day tried to put a good face on the tribulations they suffered. Life was to be lived and got on with.

When Eugene Downing published his reminiscences in the Irish language (*La Niña Bonita agus an Róisín Dubh*, An Clóchomar Tta, Baile Átha Cliath 1986) interest in the Irish participation in the International Brigades was stirring after decades of disregard, and defamation from pulpit and press. The account by the participant Michael O'Riordan (1979) drew attention, and Seán Cronin's biography of Frank Ryan (1980) was well received.[3] To date, over 40 memorials to the memory of the *brigadistas* have been erected on the island, twelve in Belfast alone. Eugene's memoir will become part of that tradition of commemoration and a reminder that 1930s Ireland was more than the green 'sceptred isle' married to Catholicism, but equally a country intensely interested in, and divided by, international politics.

Barry McLoughlin
Vienna
March 2023

CHAPTER I

SOME REFLECTIONS ON IRELAND

'There is no freedom without the freedom of the working class'

They were long days to be lying there in bed all day in a hospital ward – with nothing to do and no visitors. And there's nothing better for a bout of thinking or remembering than lying in bed all day – and not inclined to read anything much either. The silence means that you've a lot of time to think. Thoughts and images run through your mind like an old film with its own running commentary.

I was born with the sound of bombs and bullets in my ears. I'd had a ring-side seat at some of the huge military funerals of the most famous men in Ireland. When I was just three years of age, my mother and I walked one day to Carnew Street, Oxmantown Road, where her brother Greg Murphy lived. When we reached North Circular Road there was a barricade blocking the street and I remember my mother lifting me in through the door of a cab and someone on the other side grabbing hold of me. My mother followed in and the cab moved off. This is the oldest memory I have and it happened in 1916, just at the beginning of the Easter Rising. I didn't understand then, the way I do now, that my uncle Greg was active in the 1916 Rising.

I still remember the funeral of Thomas Ashe making its way through the streets of Dublin and my father lifting me up onto his shoulders so that I could see the cortège passing by. And later again, all of the other big public funerals that followed; they really affected me as a child. The heavy tread of the marching music, the slow solemn footsteps, the respectful silence of the crowd, and the sight of the cortège itself: all rich sustenance to the childish imagination.

We were living at 2 Cuffe Street. At that time Redmond's Hill was just around the corner. Redmond's Hill was a very narrow, congested area with room for just one tram line. The traffic had to slow down as it passed through there and, unsurprisingly the Volunteers were very keen on ambushing lorries full of Black and Tans whenever they came into the area. It was the best point in town to ambush them as their lorries had to slow to a stop almost at this point. The Volunteers had a variety of good escape routes from this point also because you had Bishop Street, Cheater's Lane, and Digges Street all adjacent to the area, and many tenements nearby also. Redmond's Hill was known as the 'the Dardanelles' back then. In fact, I myself got my first ever 'injury' in the Dardanelles. I was petting a dog one day there when he bit my hand. On the advice of the people who gathered around me, with my other hand, I grabbed a quick hold of skin on both sides of the bite in case the blood spurted out on the ground. 'Ah, Gawd help him! A dawg's afther bitin' him! He should get that "cawtherised" – g'wan into the chemist an' tell him yeh want it "cawtherised".' I ran into the nearest chemist in Wexford Street. 'Show me it', the chemist says. I released my grip slowly and carefully but there was no there was no sign of a cut and no blood to be seen!

The Civil War started. Initially the Volunteers took over the Four Courts. One morning my father and I were watching them down there as they were erecting barbed wire all around inside the railings. We were standing directly underneath a side window where they'd placed sandbags with rifles propped out between them. The man on guard duty inside called out to us outside and told us to move out a bit as we were so close to the walls of the building that he couldn't see us properly, and we were out of his range of vision. Initially, the new army of the Free State attacked the Four Courts and I saw the smoke and flames rising into the sky. I saw it from a back window in our room in Cuffe Street. A group of women gathered in the hallway of the tenement and they were very frightened at what was happening, their shawls draped tightly over their heads with fear. 'It's all over to Devileera!' I heard one of the women saying. 'It's all over to Devileera!'

The 'lyings in state' began and the big funerals began again. I saw Harry Boland laid out in St Vincent's Hospital. Ironically, the film *The Melody of Death* with Edgar Wallace was showing in the Metropole at the time, I remember.

A middle-aged woman lived close to us. Although her son hadn't been involved in any way with the fighting prior to this, he'd joined the new Free State Army. He'd finally managed to get some work. Although he had barely any training worth talking about, he still took part in the attack on the Four Courts, and he was shot in the head and died: Richard Reid was his name. On the morning of the funeral, I was playing with a group of boys on the path outside the house. A young girl was in the hallway of the tenement, I remember, and she was throwing a ball against the wall and singing a rhyme to herself: 'plainy, clappy, rolly, foldy, hippy, tippy, a jellybag and a basket.'[1]

Next thing I heard someone saying: 'I told him to keep his head down.' The mother of the dead man came outside and all the neighbours gathered around her trying to comfort her. She was weeping wretchedly, keening her son, and crying out in a heartbroken voice: 'I'll never see me poor Dickser again! I'll never see me poor Dickser again!' This last sentence haunted me, I remember. I was full of the Catechism back then – the nuns in Clarendon Street had made sure of that – and it was clear to me that she would see her son again when she herself died. But I've often thought about that woman said that day in the years since; she was a non-literate woman so you couldn't say that books had weakened her faith. And yet, despite this, she didn't believe in her heart that she'd ever see her son again.

The Free State Government initiated a new law that gave it the right to execute people if they were found carrying arms. Four young men were arrested carrying guns and they were executed on the 17 September 1922. A week later, Erskine Childers was shot for the same reason. On the afternoon prior to his father's execution, his son, also named Erskine, came into the bicycle shop that my uncle William Murphy owned in Rathmines and he cried his heart out with grief.

The split between both sides in the Civil War was clear even in our schoolroom with Sister Mary Paul (from Kerry) on the Republican side and Sister Mary Carmel on the Free State side – and even within the people's families, the same hostilities where there. This was the era of the snipers: the 'chimbley-pot fighters', as the slum women called them. It was around about then that they began to teach Irish in the schools. I remember that I paid sixpence a week to the Christian Brothers and every pupil paid whatever they could afford, for the classes. A short while later and we didn't need to pay anything for the classes anymore. I suppose the new government took the responsibility of teaching Irish upon themselves from then on. As regards the Irish language the monitors were learning the language themselves at night and teaching it then during the day. I remember Spider Doherty from Tipperary, a teacher in Francis Street, writing on the blackboard whatever Irish he'd learned just the night before: 'An bad, in aice an bháid, ar an mbád; Bean, mná, mnaoi, mná, ban, mnáibh.' ('The boat, near the boat, on the boat; Woman, women, of the woman, o woman, of the women, o women.')

Normally, we never took any notice of the vocative case. After all, who'd be addressing a boat – other than a fool?

Kevin's Street Technical School

In 1928 I started in the technical school in Kevin's Street where Tadhg Mac Firbisigh was teaching Irish part-time. In addition to teaching English and Maths he was also training to be a solicitor in his spare time. Pearse was Tadhg's big hero. Not only did he did we all have *Iosagán* off by heart but he would read us plays and essays by Pearse also.

Sometimes he read us out plays that were being produced in the Abbey, and performed the dialect of each character in the play. He was reading to us like this one day when suddenly, he stopped and said: 'I see now,' he says, 'that this character is a Galway man and I was talking with a Kerry accent just now.' And without the slightest difficulty, he switched to the correct accent straight away. On another occasion he was reading *The Man of Destiny* by Shaw when he came to a particular piece in the text and stopped and thought quietly to himself for a few minutes. Apparently he thought that that particular section of the play wasn't suitable for us. 'You can have a small break now', he says. Naturally enough the whole class was bursting with curiosity to know what piece he'd left out but we couldn't find out. He had a great fondness for Keats and we all knew *Ode to a Nightingale* off my heart.[2] Tadhg had a good sense of humour, also. One day, one of the boys decided to play a trick on him before he came into the classroom. He went up to the top of the room and put on small bent pin on his chair, disguising it beneath a piece of paper. When Mac Firbisigh arrived in, he was angry about something that had happened outside however and gave out stink to us for a few minutes while standing directly in front of the desk, the chair with the pin directly behind him. Naturally enough the prankster decided that this mightn't be the best time to play a trick on the master and when he thought the teacher wasn't looking, he crept up to the front and quickly grabbed the pin back again. The master turned around and caught him and his eyes widened in surprise. 'What's that in your hand?', he says. The boy opened his hand and showed him the tack and the piece of paper affixed to it as a frightened silence descended on the room. 'You could have heard a pin fall', so to speak! Next thing, Tadhg Mac Firbisigh burst out laughing, as did the whole class. A few seconds later, without any mention of whatever had angered him in the first place or to the pin, the master went on with his lessons.

Tadhg encouraged us to learn definitions off by heart the likes of: 'a logarithm is the index of the power to which the base must be raised in order to give the required number.' He also wore spats sometimes, a habit that was very rare then, even amongst the upper class; and other times, he wore golf pants. He knew a lot of the Guards (Na Gardaí Síochána, the Irish police force) very well, and it was from them that he got permission for us to use their handball ally in the yard at Kevin Street Station. He told us a story one day about one guard from Kevin Street that he wasn't on good terms with, however. He and this Guard had an argument outside the Gate Theatre one night and Tadhg was arrested and brought down to the station. The guard accused him of impeding him while in his line of duty and using foul language, apparently. Whether Tadhg had impeded him in this way, I'm not sure, but that bit about the bad language was definitely a lie. Anyway, once the guard realised who he'd arrested, he didn't pursue the case any further. The moral of Tadhg's story was this: If he'd been some poor unknown person who'd had 'no friend in court' that night, he'd have stood no chance whatsoever. Now that I think back on it, there was a touch of anti-semitism about the odd thing he said. He'd make reference sometimes to the big shops in Dublin and he'd say that 'they were owned by the Jews'. Mind you, he never explained to us what difference, if any, it'd have made to the low-paid workers of these establishments if they'd been employed by people of another religion.

Years later, he was chairperson of *The Board of Referees* and, apparently, he was very tough altogether on the workers receiving unemployment benefit. He was questioning an unemployed man one day when the man said that he was always out walking the streets looking for work. 'What about ___?', asks Tadhg mentioning such-and-such a company? 'There's a strike on there', the man says.

'That's not what I asked you', Tadhg says. 'Did you call in there looking for work? They're looking for staff there.'

'I wouldn't pass the picket line', says the man.

Whatever unemployment benefit that poor man had been receiving prior to this – and it would have been pretty low at the time – it was stopped straight away. I suppose that Mac Firbisigh had lost all the idealism of youth by that stage of his life.

Learning History

I didn't have much interest in history when I was at school. All it consisted of – the way I saw it – was a list of meaningless dates with no obvious pattern to them. But when you are unhappy with the way the world is, you get curious about it. What does history mean? Why all the social problems? The millionaire doesn't waste his time tormenting himself with such serious questions but the poor man is forever asking questions: 'What is the stars?'

Although the Censorship of Publications Act was in place back then, there was no censorship of political or philosophical books. Therefore, although *Labour in Irish History* by James Connolly wasn't available in public libraries; I suppose because it had yet to be published in hardback form. Writers such as Lenin and Bukharin were available on the shelves, and it was through reading books of this type that I moved more in the direction of Marxism. In 1931, Chris Ferguson opened a bookshop titled *The Workers' Bookshop* on 33 Winetavern Street. The shop was located at the top of the street, and there were two second-hand clothes shops on either side of it: *Mrs Murphy has cast off clothes.* The Church of Adam and Eve was at one end of the street while Christchurch was at the other, and sandwiched between them was the *Workers' Bookshop* which was spreading Marxism. Chris Ferguson was a good public speaker, and he was someone who could enthuse a crowd. At that juncture time, he was trying to organise various groups of the unemployed. At a meeting on Cathal Brugha Street he showed the crowd a photo that had appeared in one of the newspapers showing a bishop blessing soldiers' bayonets somewhere. 'And why these bayonets here?,' says Chris dramatically, 'bayonets used for the tearing out of humans innards and the Bishop shakes holy water on them?'

I bought a copy of the *Communist Manifesto* one day in Chris's shop and read it for the first time. After I'd read that book and *Labour in Irish History*, it was as if I had finally seen the light. The smashing of statues and icons began, and long-held views were jettisoned mercilessly and without regret. Here was the key that unlocked the gates of history and there was a god in the Kremlin who was the beacon of knowledge for the working classes of the world, a man who had the answer to every question and problem: It was all that simple.

The class war was the principal driving force within society. It was a war where one group sought to cling to an older, out-of-date system while another tried to destroy the system and replace it with a new and modern system more suited to the developments that had occurred in the modes of production. It was in a similar way that capitalism itself had emerged across the world, from the struggle within the feudal system between the feudal lords and the new emergent class: those makers and producers of goods and the merchants. By the same token, capitalism was out of date because of the developments that had taken place in the modes of production. Socialism would emerge from this struggle; that is to say, the nationalisation of modes of production, distribution, and exchange.

The empathy that Marx and Engels had shown towards the Irish cause helped strengthen my faith in their theories. For example, this was what Engels wrote after visiting Ireland in 1855:

> Gendarmes, priests, lawyers, officials, landlords in numbers to gladden the eye ... It would be difficult to understand how all these parasites live were it not for the corresponding contrast of the peasants' poverty.

The Revolutionary Workers' Groups (RWG)

After Fianna Fáil came to power in 1932, the headquarters of the Revolutionary Workers' Groups (from which emerged the Communist Party of Ireland in the following year) was situated at 206, Pearse Street, a few hundred yards from the Queen's Theatre. It was here that I went one night to join the Revolutionary Workers' Groups. By coincidence, Jim Prendergast was there that night too. We'd known one another from when we were young lads. The link between us back then had been for swapping comics such as *Magnet, Gem* and *Wizard,* but we hadn't run into each other for a number of years. But that night in Pearse Street, both of us – now teenagers – met up again by chance. Before long, we were swapping books of all types. We had the same taste in books and liked books relating to politics and economics where the authors put a human shape on various theories and philosophies that were then current: the likes of Jack London, H. G. Wells, Patrick McGill, George Bernard Shaw, and Theodore Dreiser. Writers like these were a big influence on us and we hadn't any hesitation about reading Chesterton and Belloc also to balance the story either. In those days, we got all our new ideas and theories from books that were completely contrary to the education we'd received up until then; ideas that eventually meant we abandoned what we'd learned as youngsters completely.

Back then, the leaders of the (Irish) Communist Party had a habit of being heavily critical of certain writers and in general it can be said that their views were narrow and sectarian for the most part. The worst 'put-down' anyone could get was to be categorised as 'bourgeois'. When Cyrano De Bergerac was showing in the Gate Theatre, myself and Prendergast went to see it, and we never heard the end of it for a long time afterwards! We were accused of acting in a 'bourgeois' way by going to see the play! (Interestingly, it seems that King Alfonso XIII's nickname was Narizotas, because he had a long nose! He was obviously the Cyrano de Bergerac of Spain!)

I remember hearing Jim Larkin Jnr[3] saying once that if even one person got as much pleasure out of Ruby Ayers[4] as another got from Shakespeare, then that meant that Ruby Ayers was as good Shakespeare. Prendergast had the book *The Science of Life* by H. G. Wells in his office one day and Jim Larkin says to him dismissively: 'H. G. Wells – the Edgar Wallace[5] of science.' His statement annoyed Prendergast. We considered writers such as Wells as liberators of the mind even if they weren't actually Marxists.

As for the membership of the [Revolutionary Workers'] Groups, they didn't really need tradespeople to join as they already had a good few of them. There were at least two or three people from each of these trades in the various groups: carpenters, plasterers, printers, plumbers. The Groups included railway workers, coopers from Guinness's brewery, a cinema operator (who'd later be Lord Mayor of Dublin during the 1940s). There was a carter, a plater, a tinsmith, and a bartender. The members also included former soldiers from the Free State Army, in addition to former members of the Irish Citizens Army.

Following the foundation of the [Irish Communist] Party in 1933, there was a scattering of lower middle-class people and intellectuals on the fringes of the organisation. An actress from the Abbey Theatre was initially a member but she left after a couple of months. Other sympathisers included the artist Harry A. Kernoff, the poet Lyle Donaghy, and Captain Jack White who helped a great deal with the foundation and training of the Irish Citizen Army prior to the Easter Rising. Outside of Dublin, there was a strong group in Kilkenny among the coalminers there, where the *Irish Miners' and Quarry Workers' Union* was active; a union that had the Party member, Nicholas Boran, as its secretary.

The primary activity the different groups were involved in was selling the weekly newspaper *The Workers' Voice*, and magazines such as *Russia Today* at public meetings and by going from house to house.

'Would you like to buy a copy of *Russia Today*?', Prendergast asked at one house.

'No. Not today, thank you,' says the woman of the house. I was fairly good at selling newspapers and magazines but I was told unkindly – in case I got a swelled head, I suppose – that people felt sorry for me because I had such a hungry or emaciated look about me! Another responsibility of ours was organising protests on behalf of the unemployed. There were always difficulties in relation to the printing of the newspaper because the clergy used to put the frighteners on the printers and the printers would give up printing material for us after a while. In this struggle between the rich and the poor, everyone knows where the clergy stand. Sixteen printers in total refused to print *The Worker's Voice* and so for a while it was actually printed in Glasgow. Eventually, after a few years we got our own printing machine in Connolly House. Later again, the Republican Congress had their own print works or press known as *The Co-op Press* under the direction of Frank Ryan where they published their own newspaper *The Republican Congress*, and it was there that the *Voice* was also printed. This latter print works was in St Anthony's Place on Gardiner Row.

We did all the typesetting by hand at the time, but the Republican Congress had its own linotype. On one occasion Frank Ryan arrived into the printing works in Connolly House. He was stressed and in a hurry. He gave me something for printing that had already been type-set at the Congress in St Anthony's Place.

'This is the stuff you've been waiting for,' he says.

'What stuff ?', says I, 'we're not waiting for anything.'

'Well,' he says, 'I did without my lunch to bring this and it's not urgent after all! I'll go upstairs to spit out my venom on Brian O'Neill, the sanguinary illegitimate. Put English on that!'

If I remember rightly, about 1,000 copies of the *Worker's Voice* were printed weekly, so its circulation was very poor really. We wouldn't have frightened anyone, such was our influence on the public – one would have thought anyway. This didn't diminish the hostility on all sides to our activities, however. Based on the venomous attacks we had to deal with, you'd have sworn we had an enormous influence on the Irish population and that a Bolshevik revolution was only just around the corner. The headquarters at Connolly House was attacked and severe damage done to the building. The Worker's College at 63 Eccles Street was also attacked at one stage.

The Worker's College

This initiative was set up so that workers could attend lectures on the history of their own class and the trade unions, politics, and economics. One occasion a row erupted between a member of the Party named Lily O'Neill and Peadar O'Donnell on some issue or other. The argument concluded with O'Donnell's comment that: 'Anyway the O'Neills and the O'Donnells were always at loggerheads!'

A range of people gave lectures on different topics at the Worker's College, amongst them Frank Ryan. He spoke on *The Young Ireland Movement* at one stage; I remember that the writer Donn Piatt was present when Frank gave his lecture. One night, a young man spoke up out of the audience and asked the following: 'What provision is made for a man's soul under communism?' The room erupted in a burst of laughter, but Peadar interrupted this by explaining that it was important to distinguish between people who used religion to put a spell over or betray the working class and the working class themselves who were honest and serious about their religious beliefs.

The Workers' Defence Corps

The Workers' Defence Corps were set up because of the various attacks on buildings and events. Vincent Poole, a former member of the Citizen's Army was involved in this organisation. He was a brother of the Fenian, Joseph Poole, executed in Richmond Prison in 1883. The leaders of the Communist Party didn't like this organisation, however, and it went into decline after a while. The Party didn't like that the Corps was an illegal grouping and they didn't want an armed wing to their organisation; this would have put the Party itself in a precarious position.

Despite its low sales *The Worker's Voice* had readers that you wouldn't have expected. Early in 1933, the *Voice* published a letter from writer Seosamh Mac Grianna[6] which was critical of an earlier review in the newspaper. It was difficult to work out exactly what Mac Grianna was getting at – based on his letter – as the opinions expressed in it were slightly vague and off-kilter, but he included the following sentences which are clear enough: 'I hold communist opinions and am an agnostic…The race-culture of the Gael is pagan and not Catholic.'

Bill Gannon called into the print-room in Connolly House one night a bit drunk and noisy. 'Are you happy now that I'm not a bourgeois anymore?', he calls out. 'I'm flat broke. I'm finally a member of the proletariat.' Gannon was directing his words at Joe Troy, and it was obvious that he was given him daggers about something but whatever it was – Joe regretted it now and said nothing. It was afterwards that I found out what was behind the whole thing. In 1934, when people were being chosen by the Party leaders to attend the Lenin School[7] in Moscow, Bill's name had been put forward before the committee. But Troy had opposed his nomination however because Gannon was a businessman at the time with his own company and had a number of people employed driving lorries for him. He wasn't technically a member of the working class therefore, according to Marxist principles. The discussion of nominations and the decision regarding who was selected for the school in Moscow was supposed to be kept private but despite this, someone revealed the details of the meeting and everyone soon knew what was decided about Bill's nomination. Poor Bill was dogged by bad luck during his life. He lost his wife to tuberculosis and was left with young children to rear by himself. Then he lost his house. Eventually he was completely broke, no doubt about it. Unfortunately for Bill, the chance to attend the Lenin School came around too early for him.

The Communist Party of Ireland

The Communist Party of Ireland was originally founded in secret. We didn't want to needlessly attract the attention of the mob to ourselves. A room was booked at 5 Leinster Street for the original foundation meeting (June 1933), under the guise of holding a Pioneer (Catholic association against alcohol) meeting there. When word got out what the meeting-room had been booked for in reality the people who rented out the meeting-rooms were very angry about the way the trick that had been played on them.

A few days after the meeting, Jim Prendergast had to return the meeting-room key to a house on Upper Merrion Street. I went with him and waited across the road for him as he went up and knocked on the door of the house. A middle-aged woman opened the door and the minute he handed her the key, she shouted out to a Guard who was directing traffic a short distance away. Prendergast ran back to me and we got out of there as quickly as we could; luckily, we escaped unscathed from that little incident!

Soon after this, in 1934, Jim Prendergast was sent to the Lenin School in Moscow along with a small group of people that included Betty Sinclair.[8] He wrote to me a few times from there and sent me a copy of *Anti-Dühring* by Frederick Engels as a present. I'm ashamed to admit that I later sold my copy in addition to a number of other books when money was tight: It's a hard life.

Connolly House under Siege

For three days in March 1933 Connolly House at 64 Great Strand Street, the headquarters of the Revolutionary Workers' Groups, was under siege from the dregs of the city. During the day the attacks on us eased off, but violent and aggressive crowds gathered again come nightfall trying to smash their way into the building and set it on fire.

In the end, all the violence meant that we who were defending the building had no choice but to give way and escape from across the roofs of some local building adjacent to it. On the night of Wednesday, 29 March 1933, the final assault took place on the building – an assault that had begun on the previous Monday and that lasted intermittently for the full two days in between. Come afternoon, Bill McGregor managed to get into the building with some food for ourselves who'd formed the 'garrison' inside. We'd fortified the entrance with big blocks of timber nailed into the floor just inside the main door in case the crowd outside rushed it and tried to smash their way in. This meant that the entrance to the building that Bill had to squeeze through – and in a hurry – was very narrow, but he managed to get into us somehow all the same. On the way into us, he let a few eggs fall on the ground and someone said laughing that we'd have scrambled eggs for our supper that evening! Later that night, no-one could get in or out of the building because the street outside was mobbed with the baying crowd. We'd to keep a close eye all the while on the back door of the building in case anyone tried to break in from an adjacent furniture factory to the left-hand side of us. We also had to keep a continuous watch from the back windows of the first floor of the building as they were situated right over the factory yard. One of us had to guard the roof of the building at all times because this area too was accessible from some nearby roofs. Strangely enough, the front door that led to the street outside was the safest area of all, when it came down to it.

In the darkness outside that evening, the police were unrecognisable from the crowd, and they seemed to be more worried about the free movement of traffic through Capel Street and Swift's Row than they were about removing the lawbreakers and rioters outside the building. During the night, many of rioters received minor injuries from the 'ammunition' (including bits of glass, timber, and stone) that they themselves had gathered up and attacked us with from outside. Donal O'Reilly was in charge of our group inside; he'd been sent home during the Easter Rising years earlier as he was considered too young to take an active part in it. At about 10.30pm that evening, some of the mob managed to smash their way through the gates of the furniture factory next door and forced their way into the building via the rear, and the situation became very dangerous. It looked as if we couldn't keep them out much longer and Joe Troy fired a shot in the direction of our attackers to try and slow them down, injuring someone in the knee. That delayed the mob for a short while. Next thing, the rioters gathered up broken bits of brick, timber, and glass which were scattered all around the factory yard, made a big pile of stuff against the front door, and attempted to set fire to the building. Burning bits of timber were shoved in through the letterbox of the front door from the street outside, and shortly after this, the fire brigade arrived on the scene. Things were so dangerous now that we realised we couldn't hold out any longer, and it was just a question of time before they forced their way into the building. We'd no option but to retreat to the loft at the top of the building and escape through the skylight there.

Brian O'Neill and Christy Clarke were out on the roof already with their guns ready to protect our escape route. Downstairs Charlie Gilmore (George's brother) was armed with a Colt pistol, and he worked to cover our back. Given that there were at least seven of us there trying to get out, it just showed how self-controlled we were really – i.e., that no-one was killed that night despite the ferocity with which we were being attacked. Most of us escaped by crossing over onto the roof of the Saint John's Ambulance Brigade Hall, which luckily enough was very close to us; a building we now sought refuge in instead. Tommy Watters followed myself and two other lads across the roofs of a series of buildings towards Capel Street, and eventually we climbed down again into a yard behind a shop on that same street. Our only way out onto the street was to go through a shop or a house there, so we knocked on the back door of one place. A low-sized, fat, Italian man opened the door. We were at the back of a fish and chip shop. Tommy explained the situation to him and that we just wanted to get through, out onto the street at the front. He just told us to wait where we were for a minute and closed the door again. We weren't too sure what was going to happen then, but sure enough, within a few minutes the man was back and told us to come into the shop, and to sit down at one of the tables there. We did as he said, and he served us fine meal while we listened to the racket still going on outside. Then we headed back out into the 'storm' again. Great Strand Street and the corner of Capel Street were both crowded with people, shouting, and screaming. We made our way through them unnoticed but then one of our group ran into a man whom he just knew to see – a man who didn't know that his pal had any connection with the Revolutionary Workers' Groups. He told us excitedly all about the battering that the 'Reds' were getting up the road. We listened to this fellow for a few minutes all happy looking, as much as to say that we were thrilled too to hear this great news. Then we disappeared in the direction of the quays, and we all went home. The same mob marched through the city again a few days later and on passing Unity Hall they threatened to destroy that building as well. Given that this hall was just a union headquarters (Workers' Union of Ireland) and nothing else, it just shows the anti-democratic character underpinning the violence against us at this juncture.

Once the riot was over a group of us went to headquarters to see the destruction at Connolly House for ourselves and Denis Larkin (Young Jim's brother) took photographs of the various rooms where everything was broken and destroyed. I was delighted to see that the electric brake lamp I'd installed above the main door just a few weeks earlier had survived the riot unscathed. I like to think that it was because of my excellent handiwork that it survived. The Blueshirts and the city's dregs were the main protagonists of this attack on us but, needless to say, there were some honest people amongst them too who'd been influenced by the malicious lies and exaggerated talk of the clergy. The following is an example of the type of thing I have in mind, and it occurred just a few years after the attack on Connolly House. Brian O'Neill was to give a lecture one night on the subject of the Paris Commune. That same night Barney McGinn and I were in the Pro-Cathedral in Marlborough Street where a Mission was being held. The priest made a bitter reference to the terrible lecture that was being held that night in the holy city of Dublin. 'We hear,' he says, 'that Brian O'Neill is the name of the speaker tonight, but I have my doubts about that. I prefer to believe that it's Isaacson or Levinsky or something like that is his real name.' And then, in a voice that was low and severe and laced with sarcasm he said, 'WHOEVER HE IS, HE SHOULD BE THROWN OUT INTO THE LIFFEY!' Maybe the public were wising up to things at this stage, however, because this priest's attempt to rally the troops to violence failed.

Bodenstown 1931

I have two memories of Bodenstown. The first relates to an incident that happened there in 1931. That year the Cumann na nGaedheal government banned any trains going to Bodenstown and the army took over the graveyard there. Despite this ban thousands of people turned up and the commemoration went ahead as normal with Peadar O'Donnell giving the graveside oration. Once the oration was over and as the soldiers, the armoured cars, and the mounted police were leaving, the 'republican masses' were lined up on either side of the road screaming at them, cursing them, and spitting at them. One mounted soldier was moving around the edge of the crowd, and you could see that he was in a real temper. Someone standing next to me shouted something insulting at him and he got really angry. He pulled firmly on the horse's reins as if to drive it forward onto his tormentor, but just as suddenly again he came to himself and retreated. I had some sympathy for these poor soldiers as they had no choice but to put up with the sarcastic jibes and abuse thrown their way while, at the same time, maintaining self-control in a tense situation; at the end of the day they were members of the working-class themselves. As it turned out, a by-election was being held in the area and later that day Paddy Hogan, the Minister for Agriculture, spoke at a meeting in Naas. He was a very good public speaker and what he said that day was interesting: 'There are two diseases the people of this country are suffering from,' he says, 'one of them is Foot-and-Mouth disease and the other is Fianna Fáil.'

Peadar O'Donnell, Berlin, 1930

11

Irish delegates at the Communist Peasants International, Berlin, March 1930, Peadar O'Donnell is in the middle

Frank Ryan

The next memory I have relates to Frank Ryan[9] and the Republican Congress. I saw Frank Ryan for the first time sometime towards the end of the 1920s. He was speaking at an anti-imperialist meeting in Foster Place, College Green, in Dublin. When he'd finished speaking he pulled out a Union Jack and set fire to it. Another time I saw him carrying a walking stick in order to protect himself against the CID (Criminal Investigation Department, secret police) who were forever interrupting him and harassing him. The Republican movement was at a low ebb at the time. Normally Frank began any of his speeches at public meetings by speaking in Irish initially. I remember one exception to this, however. A meeting was being held close to Berkeley Road, next to Mountjoy Jail.

There was just a very small crowd there. This was at a time when the Republican movement was so weak that Peadar O'Donnell would later say of this period: 'Frank Ryan was the Republican movement.' Ryan didn't speak at the Berkeley Road meeting, however, because he'd arranged to go to the gates of Mountjoy Jail which was just a hundred yards or so further down the road. Just as he was getting to speak, a Garda Inspector said to him in a hostile way that no gathering would be allowed outside the prison. Frank turned away from him without a word; he didn't look at the Guard even, never mind respond to him.

'If you're looking for trouble, Ryan,' the Inspector says angrily, 'you'll get it!' Frank stood still as a statue but remained silent. The platform was surrounded by guards and detectives at this stage but, next thing, he climbed up onto the back of the cart and started to speak.

'I want to tell you what the Inspector has just said to me. The Inspector says he will use any force he thinks necessary to stop the meeting.'

The guards and detectives suddenly jumped and knocked him off the cart. A detective whacked the horse on the rump and the cart and driver had no option but to move on to a different spot a few hundred yards from the prison gates, down closer to Dorset Street. The guards were happy enough to let the speeches go ahead down there. That was the first time that I ever heard Frank make a speech in English. He knew that he wouldn't have time to explain to the crowd how the police inspector had threatened him. They didn't begin teaching the Irish language schools until 1923 and so the vast majority of his audience wouldn't have had any knowledge of the language at this point. There was a big difference between the small ineffectual meeting that day (where there are more detectives than there were listeners) and the enormous crowds in College Green following Fianna Fáil's victory in the General Election of 1932 and the release of the political prisoners. In his speech on this occasion, Frank said that he'd been certain the people of Dublin wouldn't let us down. A huge roar of joy went up from the thousands in the crowd at that gathering.

Frank Ryan understood that one had to make a distinction between the working class and the establishment. Therefore it was decided to put an end to the attacks on former British soldiers that happened every year on 'Poppy Day' (11 November). He extended a hand of friendship towards these former soldiers instead. In fact, he managed to organise a parade at one stage where both Republicans and former First World War soldiers marched together. Ryan's aim was to put an end to the senseless violence between different groups of the working class that had occurred on such days.

It was this radically new outlook of his that lay behind the Republican Congress set up in 1934. Some in the IRA were moving closer to James Connolly's philosophy and they were thrown out of the IRA as a consequence and considered 'communists' from then on. In 1935, the Wolf Tone Commemoration Committee issued a statement welcoming every organisation to the commemorations albeit that they wouldn't be allowed to carry flags. Everyone understood that this rule had been instituted primarily against the (Republican) Congress and the Communist Party of Ireland.

Myself and another member of the [Communist] Party decided to camp in Bodenstown on the Saturday night prior to the commemoration. We are asked to bring our flag with us in case it was confiscated by one of the stewards when we were on the train the following day. We cycled to Bodenstown and hid the flag in the tent. The following morning we saw Frank on the road putting up posters relating to the Congress on a number of telegraph poles. 'Good morning lads', he said in greeting. When it came time to gather in the park, we unfurled the flag and held it high over where Party members had organised themselves into marching formation. On the other side of the park, Frank and various members of the Republican Congress did the same as us. No sooner had we raised our flag than a group of stewards arrived over and spoke to Seán Murray and Young Jim Larkin. After a short discussion, we lowered our flag again.

The exact opposite happened on the other side of the park, however, where Frank and his comrades were resisting the efforts of the stewards to get them to lower their flag. A brief fracas ensued on that side. Eventually the stewards gave up trying to enforce the rules and we decided to leave anyway. We re-grouped outside and decided to have own commemoration right there and then in the park. What happened that day would have consequences, however. During an informal meeting in Connolly House that night on our return from Bodenstown a bitter debate ensued about what happened that day, the various comrades in heated discussion with one another. A number of people disagreed with how things turned out that day and left the Party because of it.

Explaining the outcome of that meeting and defending the decision, Brian O'Neill, editor of the *Worker's Voice*, later said: 'How would it look in the newspapers that the party had been in conflict with the IRA?' My interpretation of his words was that the Party leaders were looking over their shoulders all the time at London and Moscow. Frank Ryan never criticised the party publicly about what happened that day, but privately he said to a number of people that 'the Communist Party let us down'. When street mobs started attacking Communists and when Connolly House was set on fire, Frank Ryan was disgusted.

He stood up to the Animal Gang[10] also when they directed their attention towards him personally; his courage never failed him. He was speaking at a meeting in Cathal Brugha Street when a group of these street thugs appeared with their knuckle-dusters and razorblades, and all the rest of it. They were intent on causing trouble at this event, needless to say, but Frank finished his speech and came down from the platform. Suddenly a hostile voice shouted out aggressively from the crowd: 'A question for you!' The trouble was about to kick off. Frank went straight back up onto the platform and faced this questioner without the slightest hint of fear, however. And he knew full well that he had no protection at all if they attacked him right there and then. There were just a few people present who were on his side and they would easily have been routed by this mob. 'What's the question?' Ryan said, hands on hips. 'Are you a communist?' The crowd was on tenterhooks waiting for his response. Frank could have said in all truth, 'I'm not a communist,' but that wouldn't have satisfied them. Frank threw back his head and shoulders in that dignified way of his and spoke out boldly and enthusiastically – espousing his own personal philosophy as relating to the socialism and the working class. And he finished his short speech with a challenge: 'Now, if that is communism, then I am a Communist,' he said, climbing down from the platform again. The listening crowd went silent; they were completely mollified.

He'd spoken to them in that completely open and honest way of his and had such an effect on them that they were left stunned almost. I don't know what the 'tough guys' thought of Frank Ryan's words, but I remember that Frank left Cathal Brugha Street that day and no-one laid a finger on him. Whatever they thought of Ryan or his views, in the end, they had to respect him. Whenever Frank was speaking about something he felt was an injustice, you could feel the honesty and integrity of his anger; it was completely different from that insincere rage you often heard from the professional politician. He always spoke with a passion in his voice. He was a humane and kind person, and it was always obvious that his personal political outlook had emerged from deep within his heart. By this stage he had gone the full circuit almost – as a lone ranger: in the 1920s, almost – then, as a great hero of the Republican masses in the early-1930s – and back again, as a Socialist Republican – almost a lone ranger once again, in the end.

The following memory of Frank relates closely to myself. The Congress and the Party organised a night out in *Lamb Doyle's* in Ticknock at one stage. Sometime during the night I was drinking with a group of people in the snug. Amongst them were Frank and a friend of his from America, a Mrs O'Reilly. I wasn't sure whether I had enough money to buy drinks for everyone in our group but after a while, when I felt it was my round and emboldened by drink, I went up to the counter and called for the same again. The girl behind the bar placed the drinks on the counter and told me how much. I put my money on the counter and begin to count it out. I knew straightaway that I was short and that I didn't have enough. I was worried now. There was a lot of noise in the pub with people talking and laughing and so on, and no-one in the company had noticed the quandary I was in. The girl behind the counter was anxiously waiting for me and I was staring down at the coins as if – by pure hope – I could magic it into more money somehow. Suddenly, a voice from behind me said: 'Are you alright there? Are you in trouble?' The right amount was put on the counter and the girl took it. It was Frank. I handed whatever money I had to him, saying, 'here's your change Frank', but he just handed it back to me and we sat down again.

In January 1935, Frank was to act as a chairman at a debate being held under the auspices of the *Cumann Gaelach* (Irish Language Society) in University College Dublin. The motion for debate was whether a Socialist Government was the sole solution to Ireland's problems. Dr Coffey, the University's president banned the debate, however, 'because of the propagandist nature of the motion and because Mr Ryan was engaged in a public controversy with the Bishop of Waterford and Lismore.'[11] The O'Rahilly wrote to the newspapers at the time saying that Dr Coffey had not consulted with the University's Governing Authority on the issue – something that he should have done in his opinion. Referring to the explanation the College president gave with regards to banning the meeting he said '[it] would make the National University the laughing stock of Europe.'

When Frank was on leave from Spain in 1937 because he was injured, he was passing Trinity College one day when a man approached him. 'Are you Frank Ryan?', the man asked. 'I'm Jim Prendergast's father. He's fighting out in Spain at the moment.' On hearing this, Frank was expecting a tongue-lashing and a whole heap of criticism, and he steeled himself too for a long rant directed at him. But rather than giving out to him because his son was in danger of being killed and that Frank was the one responsible for this etc., this man shook Frank's hand instead and spoke to him in a nice, friendly way. Frank was delighted. Jim Prendergast, himself, told me this story after he had returned from Spain later that same year.

Street Activism

Seán Redmond and I often went out at night and engaged in street activism or 'street journalism' to get important messages across to the city's working class. The first path I chose to write an essential message for the working people on was close to the Post Office on Prince's Street North. On the night I went out, a Guard was standing at the corner watching me carefully, a hostile look in his eyes. I was sure that he'd be over to me for my name and address before I was finished. Writing on the path with a piece of chalk, I wrote 'There is no freedom without the freedom of the working class.' Sure enough, the Guard came over and read the statement, but he returned to his station back on the corner again without interrupting me at all. I could tell by him straight away that he was an understanding man, someone who agreed completely with the philosophy I'd expressed, and that his hostility had disappeared, as a consequence. Seán Redmond was just a short distance from me in O'Connell Street busily writing also. Our propaganda work that night didn't last very long however because shortly after we began work, it rained, and our chalk was wiped away. We weren't too worried about this, however, as we understood that the weather-clerk must be on the payroll of the forces of imperialism.

Another blow against the system, as we saw it, was writing statements and messages on the Wellington Monument in the Phoenix Park. We found it very funny to make use of the Duke in order to proclaim revolutionary messages. One evening, at dusk, I remember us working away quietly with our pieces of chalk. Our efforts that night didn't seem to have any great effect on the people however, and we didn't notice any particular change in the mood of city the following day; it wasn't as if any frightened silence descended on the authorities either as a result of our actions. There was something fairly ineffective about writing in chalk we decided, after a while, something that took from the meaning and power of the message. We needed to change our mode of propaganda.

We decided to make our next effort during the Horse Fair at Smithfield in order to communicate directly with the crowds. So we abandoned the temporary medium that was chalk this time and went with paint instead. We had additional forces on our side this time also, in the form of Mrs McGregor and Barney McGinn.[12] Given that there was an international campaign on at this time agitating for the release of Ernst Thälmann, the well-known German communist (he'd been imprisoned by Hitler), we decided to focus our energies on this case. We reminded one another also to include the two dots (umlaut) over the letter 'a' in his surname as proof that propaganda and culture can happily co-exist. It happened sometimes that well known scholars and intellectuals attended the Horse Fair. To complete our work that night, Seán Redmond, and I skipped quickly up the steps of 58 Northumberland Road, the residence of the then German Ambassador to Ireland, a Herr von Kuhlmann. Seán painted the word 'Release' on the door of the residence and I painted 'Thälmann' just underneath it. It wasn't to save time that we both wrote words on the door but rather to confuse the enemy with the two different styles of writing. (We were way ahead in those days from a strategy point of view.) The following morning everything we'd written had been wiped away, the two dots included. The authorities can work very quickly when it suits them.

The Guards didn't like these activities of ours because they were we were breaking some by-law or other even if the only penalty we suffered was that they might take your name and your address, but you wouldn't hear any more about it. Sometimes, a rude or gruff activist might refuse to give this information (name, address etc.) to show that they didn't recognise the State and a stupid and pointless fracas would be the result. We wouldn't lower ourselves to this level, however, because the way we saw it there was no useful outcome from spilling blood in such a way. More large-scale terrorism was okay but all you got from one-on-one individual battles was a sore head and it proved fruitless as regards social change.

An example of this was an incident that happened in May 1935. Kevin Blake[13] was getting ready to go to Mass one Sunday. Outside his house, a member of the IRA approached him and asked him to hide a gun for him – for a short while. Kevin went back into his house and hid the gun. After Mass he bought the *Sunday Independent*. On the front page he saw the following headline: 'DUBLIN SHOOTING: SIX SHOTS AT GARDA.' Apparently a young Garda had interrupted a group of street activists who belonged to the IRA who were out painting propaganda slogans the previous night near Earlsfort Terrace. Kevin rushed back to the house and examined the gun. It was obvious to him that it had been used very recently so he got rid of the gun straight away. For a finish, the Garda involved in the incident got a promotion and the gunmen got a prison sentence.

For a short while after the foundation of the Broy Harriers (secret policemen with Fianna Fáil sympathies), regular harassment from the police eased off somewhat. One time myself and Seán Redmond were putting up posters late at night when we heard those regular marching footsteps approaching us from behind somewhere, footsteps we were only too well-used to by then. The Broy Harrier stopped and examined our poster carefully. It was a poster for an anti-Blueshirt (semi-fascist organisation led by Eoin O'Duffy) meeting we were putting up. 'Good night lads,' the guard said, and continued on his rounds. This was a new and odd development for us and for a while I began to think I was now part of the 'establishment' and that I was as well off getting a job in the civil service! Once the threat from the Blueshirts passed off the Broy Harriers quickly turned their attentions from the right wing to the left wing again, and the honeymoon was over.

Another time we were out postering again when two detectives happened to pass us the other side of the road. They came over to us – a middle-aged man and a younger man. They waited until we had the posters up. 'Who gave you the authority to hang those posters there?', says the more senior man.

'The Republican Congress,' says I.

'Rubbish!', he says gruffly, taking out his notebook.

'You know well that the Republican Congress has no authority to permit you break the by-laws like this.'

As we always did, we politely gave the guard our details and he wrote them down carefully in his notebook. Having explained to his trainee detective how to handle dangerous matters such as this, the older man visibly relaxed, then began explaining the finer points of the law to us. Seán asked him why it was against the law to write on the road.

'That's damaging public property, that's why.' And that wasn't the only thing either.

'Suppose a passing horse was startled and someone was hurt. You'd be responsible for it.'

'Only a fascist horse would startle like that,' said Seán. 'It's not right that fascist horses would have work either, especially given how many republican horses are unemployed.' The trainee detective gave a small laugh at this but the other man was still full of the law and very serious about all relating to it. I sensed that he was probably running over umpteen laws and regulations in his mind at that very moment.

'In this case, it's up to the court to resolve that particular issue,' he said solemnly in conclusion. Anyway, I never heard that our street writings and activism ever frightened any horse. This proves that Dublin horses were always opposed to fascism – or that they were illiterate maybe!

War in Abyssinia

In October 1935, Mussolini initiated the war in Abyssinia. The Italian bishops gave their blessing to this terrible violence and Cardinal Schuster of Milan praised this campaign, which had as its aim: 'to open the gates of Ethiopia at the cost of blood to the Catholic faith and to Roman civilisation'. The blood spilt would be that of the ordinary people apparently because – for as long as Vittorio and Bruno, Mussolini's sons were safe and sound in their bomber planes pounding the Ethiopian people – the regular soldiers or the poor of Italy were dying on the ground at the same time. The wives of Italy were asked to donate their wedding rings to the state so that Mussolini could fund the war. The clergy took it upon themselves to gather the gold rings in their churches. 'The Ritual of the Marriage Ring' was the gallant title given to this form of barbarism. The Communist Party of Ireland organised public meetings against this unjust war.

Visit to the Castle

It was reported at one stage that detectives from Dublin Castle had seized leaflets that a member of the party had been handing out. The member of the party in question was an elderly man. Jim Prendergast had just returned from the Lenin School in Moscow and was full of Bolshevik enthusiasm. Off he went to Dublin Castle to complain at this turn of events. He swept me along with him on this visit. Given that I followed him reluctantly and that he was 'tornado-like' in his approach, I think that the verb 'swept' is particularly appropriate in this case. The guard at the Castle gates directed us to the detectives' section, where Prendergast gave out stink to the poor clerk in that office. Despite this lambasting from Prendergast however, the clerk kept his cool, calmly explaining that the person from whom these pamphlets had been confiscated would have to make an official complaint himself – rather than us. Prendergast went ballistic on hearing this and between banging doors in a rage and general aggression, I don't know how he left the Castle again without getting himself arrested for breach of the peace. I was sensible enough not to follow suit; you need to have a particular skill to emerge unscathed from such volatile situations. I followed Prendergast back out again like the tail of a comet.

Strikers in Mountjoy

In 1935 when the Republican Congress was quite an active organisation, there was an incident in Dublin that only served to highlight why the Congress had been founded in the first place. The workers in a number of shops owned by the company *Bacon Shops Ltd* in the Dublin city went out on strike. A picket in sympathy with the strikers was organised for this company's shops one night. Under the general umbrella of the Republican Congress, different organisations on the left were able to work together without sacrificing their independence to one another: the aim of the Congress from the first day.

Amongst the various groups who took part in this general picket were various trade unionists and republicans in addition to other sympathetic people who wished to demonstrate their moral support for the strikers. Out of more than 30 people who took part in the picket more than a dozen were arrested and received a month in prison as punishment – James Connolly's son Roddy amongst them. On Saturday, 5 January 1935, at around 7.30pm, we began to march up and down outside one of the Bacon Shops on Dorset Street shouting out: 'Strike on here', etc. After a short while, we left Dorset Street for Moore Street. The company owned another shop on this street and we made the exact same protest there. A group of Guards and detectives appeared on the scene, all of a sudden. Station Sergeant McCarthy from Store Street spoke to the people at the front of the picket.

'Who's in charge here?', he asked authoritatively.

'I'm responsible for everything', said Larry O'Connor, the chairman of the Congress's Dublin Council.

We were breaking the law, the sergeant explained, but ignoring him, we continued marching up and down the street protesting all the while. Next, the sergeant said that he was arresting all of us and that we'd have to accompany them to the station. We refused to come to the station and informed the guards that we wouldn't go quietly. The argument continued between the sergeant on the one side and O'Connor and Roddy Connolly on the other, and the guards and detectives that had surrounded us all ears and staring us down all the while. As one of the picketers said to Sergeant Mark Byrne who was also present: 'It isn't just me that you're arresting but the trade union movement itself.' Not that this over-the-top statement had any effect whatsoever on the Sergeant!

The company had another shop on Talbot Street and we now made for there, passing through Henry Street, O'Connell Street and Earl Street North, the police walking alongside us; they were happy that we were at least moving closer to the station, I suppose. On reaching Talbot Street we stopped at the shop and another bout of arguing and dispute ensued. No attempt was made to arrest us by force, and the sergeant patiently continued with his attempts to get us to come into the station in a peaceful manner. The negotiations went on for a while and eventually, the sergeant won out. In reality, it'd been clear from the very beginning that we'd end up having to go into the station. The police station was crowded when we reached it; there were more prisoners than police. It was chaotic and noisy with guards rushing in and out, telephones constantly ringing, and the prisoners talking amongst one another. Inspector Timothy Maher was saying crankily to someone on the phone: 'It doesn't matter if you're the Lord Mayor, you'll have to wait. I'm busy.' The entire police unit was busy writing everyone's name and address down. We were given the usual warning beforehand regarding 'everything you say will be written down', etc. Two girls had taken part in the picket–Cora Hughes[14] and Nellie Philbin.

Mark Byrne asked Nellie. 'So what does Nellie mean really?', he said.

'Nellie', she replied.

He gave her a dubious look. 'Isn't it short for some other name?'

'No,' she says. 'It just means "Nellie"', and he reluctantly noted her name. Once the authorities were happy that they had all the requisite information we were all released again. In the meantime, in his house on Eccles Street, Peadar O'Donnell had got wind of what was going on. On our way home, he pulled in beside us in his car. We gathered around him in Frenchman's Lane, opposite the Employment Exchange on Gardiner Street. I gave him a run-down on everything that had happened.

'Was everyone arrested?' he asked.

'Two or three people escaped.'

'It's a pity even more didn't give them the slip.' The movement was weak enough as it was without 20 people being taken in by the police.

The following morning we had a meeting to discuss the situation. What should we do when our case came to court? Should we defend ourselves without a solicitor or without employing someone to defend us? As part of our discussion, a few people proposed that we not recognise the court. The majority of our group were against this approach, however, and it was decided that we should have our own solicitor. On Monday, 7 January, our case was heard in Green Street Courthouse. The case came before District Justice Little. Ernest

Wood KC and Alec Lynn BL were defending us. The dock wasn't big enough to hold all of us – 23 defendants altogether – and extra chairs were brought in on one side of the court. We were charged with 'besetting the premises of Bacon Shops Ltd, obstructing the free passage of the thoroughfare, threatening behaviour calculated to provoke a breach of the peace, etc.'

Our defence argued that we were using the roads in a legal fashion and simply exercising our rights as citizens. It would have been difficult to find a more biased judge in relation to our case however than the one we had now. Prior to this, in many other cases, the same man had confirmed that 'there is no statutory right, and I know of no common law right, for any man, with a banner or not, to walk on the public roadway back and forward.' And 'citizens have no right to congregate in public meeting in the streets.' We had very little chance of winning with a judge like that presiding over our case.

For most of the time in court, the solicitors were concerned with boring legal questions – back and forth. Every now and then, an argument would develop between the judge and Ernest Wood, and then things would liven up slightly. When Mark Byrne was giving evidence, he made some reference to Joe Doyle, one of the prisoners at one stage. Joe didn't agree with something that one of the witnesses said about him and shouted out: 'Don't perjure yourself, Mark Byrne! Don't perjure yourself!' There was a silence in the court for a moment. Then the judge spoke slowly and deliberately, and warned him that if he didn't stay quiet 'he would commit him for six months.' And he said 'You have able people here to defend you.' The judgement in the end – guilty. As regards the 'threatening behaviour' we had to take bail or agree not to do the same thing again. We refused to agree to this and also refused to pay the fine of £5 each. Consequently, we were all imprisoned for one month.

On Saturday, 12 January, we all went down to the Bridewell to wait for the *Black Maria*. Peadar O'Donnell and Frank Ryan where there, as were other people that were sympathetic to us. While we were waiting Roddy Connolly said jokingly, 'A whole month without a woman! I can't do it!' Nelly and Cora were sent to the women's prison in Mountjoy in a private car. It was decided beforehand that Roddy and Jack Nalty would be in charge of us while we were in prison. Seán Kavanagh, the Prison Governor, accepted them as spokespeople on our behalf and following a medical exam, we were all sent to our cells. Just as we were readying to march out from the cells in military formation to the yard outside on our first morning, one of the warders gave us a gruff order. Jack Nalty turned around, looked over at the warder and quietly said: 'I'm in charge here, I give the orders.' The warder stared at him. He was stunned. It's unlikely that any prisoner had ever spoken to him like that before.

Jack Nalty (centre) with his brothers during WW1

We had lectures in the prison yard on political issues. Around this time, Hitler was trying to gain control of the Saar and a referendum was going on there; so, Roddy gave us a lecture on this subject. During one lecture it began to rain. We went up the steps of the building and into the small hallway there to shelter from the rain. Suddenly the Governor arrived in with one of his senior warders. The Governor stared at us angrily for a moment: 'Where's the warder', he says. He went out the door to the top of the steps and spotted the young man walking around the yard by himself. He turned to the other officer then and says: 'Tell him to get in here immediately', and left. He got very little satisfaction for his complaints, however. The warder came in and says nervously – 'What did he say?'

Another day, the Visiting Committee arrived at the prison, Peadar S. Doyle TD amongst them. They stood at the top of the steps looking down at us in the yard where we were gathered around Charlie Donnelly who was giving us a lecture. After a short while they left again. Of course we didn't spend all our time listening to lectures. We played skittles, handball, and oddly enough, a type of cricket as well. Over time you got more used to your days in prison life as every day follows a particular routine. I never had enough to eat in Mountjoy, and Roddy Connolly advised me to go to the doctor and ask him if I could have a pint of milk a day. The senior warder was in the room when I met the doctor and let a sudden roar out of him: 'Get your hands out of your pockets, Downing!', he shouted. It'd never occurred to me that I'd have to stand to attention in the presence of the prison doctor but I did as I was told. A few minutes later and I forgot myself again and began to slouch and he ordered me to attention again. I didn't get the milk anyway; the doctor didn't think that I needed it. Or maybe I was refused because I'd been 'disrespectful' in front of the doctor, I don't know. Charlie wrote a funny verse about this incident on a piece of paper and handed it to me the following day:

Here grass abounds 'neath city slime
There is no haste – you're doing time!

Eat it all up and chew the cud,
It's bound to do you no bloody good!

In one of the cells next to me was Jim Fox. He'd given his name as 'Foley' to the prison authorities because he was a tram conductor and didn't want to lose his job. He'd often wake me in the morning, singing at the top of his voice: 'Oh it's nice to get up in the morning *but* it's better to stay in bed!' And a big hearty laugh afterwards.

Anyway, whatever excuse he gave to the Dublin United Tramway company as to why he was absent from work for a whole month, he managed to get his job back on the trams anyway. His brother Tony Fox was killed in Spain in the fighting at Cordoba in December 1936. The priest in Inchicore refused to say Mass for him, a refusal that upset his family a great deal. On the first Sunday that we went to Mass in prison, the sermon was of much interest to us: Jesus showed his humility to his mother when he made wine of the water. This proved – according to the priest's reasoning – that it was everyone's duty to respect the State authorities and demonstrate humility towards them at all times. He directed his attention at us all the while he was saying this. He wasn't too bothered about the other prisoners by all accounts. He was trying to convince us (or that's how it looked anyway), that because Jesus had provided wine for the wedding at Cana – out of respect for his mother – that the working class should be happy with poor wages and oppression. We failed to see how both issues were linked.

Christy Clark (or 'Sniper' as he was known) told us a funny story about Seán Russell, a major figure in the IRA during the 1930s. When Christy came home from the Lenin School in Moscow, he paid Seán Russell a visit. He told him about the revolution that had taken place in Russia during 1917, the class war there and the changes that followed it, and the efforts that the working class were making to establish socialism there. 'That may be alright in Russia,' says Russell, 'but there are no classes in Ireland.'

While in prison I tried to grow a beard but as it got longer the others referred to me as Rasputin, and the beard had to go. We were eventually freed on the 15 February. On my way home through O'Connell Street it was obvious to me that the people weren't particularly delighted that I was a free man again. Everyone ignored me. Instead of falling apart, the capitalist system was still as strongly established as were the stone statues everywhere; I found this really disappointing. In the same year, 1935, Donal O'Reilly, a man who had his own political views on things, was thrown out of the (Communist) Party because of his 'political unorthodoxy'.

The Blueshirts were very active at this juncture. One night I went to a meeting of theirs in Gloucester Diamond where Paddy Belton was the principal speaker. He had people protecting him all around the platform where he was speaking. This was in July 1937. 'Can any man here say that he ever got less than eight pence an hour working for me?', he shouted. 'I pay the best rates to my workers. Is there anyone here who can say different?' Maybe Belton wasn't expecting to find a farm labourer in the Gloucester Diamond, in the heart of the slums, that night, but next minute a man spoke up from the crowd.

'I was working for you, and I got less than that!'

Belton got really angry – someone contradicting him!

'Who are you?', he says, in a temper. 'I've never seen you before! Inspector – remove that man from this meeting!' There was a strong force of Garda Síochána present that night and the Inspector as accompanied by a police sergeant made their way through the crowd towards the man who'd just spoken. As they passed by, I overheard the Sergeant say quietly to the Inspector: 'Don't mind him.' The Inspector was just as wound up as Belton was, however. 'Oh yes, I will mind him,' he says and shoved the man out to the fringes of the crowd. Belton was involved with the group who went to Spain to support General Franco and the following verse was written about him as published in *The Worker*, in September 1936:

There's a boy called Paddy Belton
With a heart that's soft and meltin'
Yet the first to face the foeman, danger scorning.
Though his feet are full of bunions
Yet he knows his Spanish onions
And he's off to Salamanca in the morning.

Tragedy in Scotland

That same year, 1937, in September, a terrible tragedy occurred in a small town in Scotland named Kirkintilloch. Ten young lads from Achill who were working as 'tatie-hokers' in the area died in a devastating fire. It was the norm at the time for thousands of Irish speakers from the Gaeltacht areas to go to England and Scotland working on the potatoes. The boys and girls detested this slave-work and all the hardship that went with it, but they had no choice, They had to earn money somehow, no matter how small the money was. What happened was that a bothy went on fire – 'a shack with beds of straw and a roof of tar'. The Solemn Mass of the Dead was said at the funerals of the ten men, amongst the attendance at which were Ministers of State. It didn't seem to occur to the Church prelates or the upper-class members of State present however that this terrible incident had reflected very badly upon themselves. They should have been ashamed and filled with guilt that these unfortunate teenagers had had no choice but to leave their native country and put up with every type of slavery and insult in a foreign country.

Writing in Irish for the newspaper *Scéala Éireann*,[15] at the time of the funerals, someone wrote: Tá olagón i mbéal na gaoithe a réabfadh an chloch ghlas. Tá Acaill ina Theach Tórraimh (There's a keening in the mouth of the wind that would tear apart the limestone rocks. Achill is a mortuary). That same year Cardinal McRory had sent more than £40,000 to the Archbishop of Toledo, in support of Franco.[16]

A Ban on Ernest Toller

Another series of thoughts was set in train while I was lying injured in that hospital in Mataró – this was when I heard that a party was being held in the Majestic Hotel in Barcelona at the time. Amongst those present were Ernst Toller[17] and Theodore Dreiser. This party took place in October 1938. I had just read the novel entitled *An American Tragedy*, a book that left-wing people had a lot of respect for at the time. But I was more interested in Ernest Toller himself, and there were two reasons for this. As I was leaving Dublin with a small group to travel to Spain on 24 March 1938, a play was being produced in the Abbey Theatre, based on a story written by Ernst Toller. Denis Johnson had adapted the story for the stage and provided it with an Irish background. *Blind Man's Buff* was the story's title and it triggered another memory relating to this famous writer. In January 1935 a meeting was held against fascism in the town hall in Rathmines under the auspices of the *Irish Labour League against Fascism*. I was asked to book the hall and make the arrangements with Mr Thunder, a member of the vocational committee at the time. Ernst Toller was due to speak at the meeting and F. R. Higgins was to act as chair for the event. Higgins was quite famous as a poet at the time and had been involved with the Abbey Theatre and was also one of the founders of the Irish Academy of Letters. For some reason Higgins pulled out of the meeting and John Breen (later Lord Mayor of Dublin during the 1940s) took on this role. Come the day of the meeting the audience was in the hall and the speakers all on stage – all except for Ernst Toller. The main speaker was nowhere to be seen, because he was still in London! Apparently Mr Dulanty, the Commissioner of the Irish Free State in London, had already indicated to Toller that he'd be allowed to speak on literary issues at the event but not on anything related to politics or against Hitler. The objective of that meeting was to protest against fascism however and the repression then taking place in Germany so the prohibition on Toller meant that he couldn't speak at the event in Dublin at all really.

Superintendent McCarthy and a large force of police were in the hall that night and an announcement was made warning everyone that if Ernst Toller appeared at the event or made any attempt to speak at it, he'd be arrested and extradited from Ireland immediately. Owen Sheehy Skeffington put forward a motion criticising the oppression and violence then occurring in Germany and it was agreed to send a delegation to Herr von Kuhlmann, the German Ambassador in Dublin, making clear our views on the issue. Supporting the motion Peadar O'Donnell said: 'My mind is in a rage at the refusal to allow Ernst Toller to speak … The deportation of a man of Toller's standing to Germany would simply mean handing him over to the axe.' The other speakers at the event – Dr A. J. Leventhal, Miss Dorothy Woodman (London), and Seán Murray – all criticised the Irish Government heavily for imposing a ban on this well-known writer. Seán Murray said, '[that] deportation was not unknown to the Government as they had already deported a man called Gralton[18] at the insistence of secret instigators opposed to his ideas.'

CHAPTER 2

THE JOURNEY TO SPAIN

When I told my parents one day in March 1938 that I was going to Aintree, Liverpool, to see the Grand National, they were surprised. I'd never been known for having any interest in horseracing before.

The night before race day I went to 32 Lower Ormond Quay, Dublin, the then headquarters of the Irish Communist Party. I met Seán Murray, Secretary of the Party there. Seán was always a happy person with big red, well-fed cheeks that would have reminded you of a Bishop. He stuck a piece of paper under my nose.

'Can you read that?'

'Easily,' I replied.

'You're chosen so. Your sight is fine.'

Seán Murray, delegate to the 7th Congress of the Communist International, Moscow 1935

I was mightily relieved to have passed this very 'strict' medical exam and deemed fit enough to go to Spain and take part in the Civil War there! There were five of us altogether, two Corkonians and three Dubliners. The Corkonians and I were new recruits, but Jack Nalty and his close friend Paddy Duff were returning to Spain having already done a tour of duty there. There'd both been injured at Cordoba in December 1936 and Paddy was wounded again in February 1937. We left the head office once we'd all our preparations done for the journey to Spain where we were going to fight on behalf of the Republic in the Civil War that began in July 1936 and was still ongoing.

'Keep your heads down!' Jim Prendergast said to us as a parting shot, going downstairs from head office. He himself had returned from Spain shortly prior to this after he'd been injured on Pingarrón Hill during the battle of Jarama, in February 1937. Off we went to get the boat at the North Wall. The boat was crowded with people whose sole concern was which horse would win the big race at Aintree. The five of us kept to ourselves sitting at a table in the corner of the bar drinking and quietly observing all the commotion around us.

The genesis of this adventure lay in a visit Jim Prendergast paid me shortly after he returned from Spain. We went for a walk around Stephen's Green, which was a habit of ours when we had any issue to discuss. Many's the hour we spent circling that Green again and again until nightfall debating political, philosophical, literary questions and other similar 'heavy-duty' issues. Back then, we thought that the revolution was only just 'around the corner' and there wasn't much time left to get everything ready for this momentous day. And yet, despite all our discussions and debates we'd hadn't convinced the working class to jettison capitalism and assume control of the means of production, distribution, and exchange for themselves. Over time, we gradually came to the conclusion that we'd got it wrong. In so far as it related to 'history', the 'Republic of Workers and Small Farmers' had never been likely or on the agenda. Therefore, when the war in Spain came along many people 'rose from the dead' who'd become sick of all the delays and stagnation of history. That clever individual by the name of De Valera had succeeded in outflanking the Left-wing movement and they were now in a limbo of sorts, as a consequence. In Spain, however, rather than chomping at the heels of history we'd be at the heart of the battle for certain. This was how I came to find myself supposedly attending the Grand National in March 1938.

After breakfast in Liverpool we went to the office of the Communist Party of Great Britain but we were so early in the morning arriving, that they hadn't opened yet. Hughie Hunter from Belfast was already there waiting patiently by himself outside. On receiving directions from officers of the party we made our way down to the public baths. Finally, we were on the coach to London! I'd a copy of Hugo's *Spanish Self-Taught* on me and tried to learn a little bit of Spanish on the journey. In an office in Litchfield Street, London, not far from St Martin's Theatre, we met Johnny Larmour, another Belfast-man who'd just returned from Spain where he'd been injured in the hand in Cordoba at the end of December 1936. He was on the committee charged with preparing the way for new recruits going out to Spain. It was arranged for us to go to Victoria Station where we'd get a weekend ticket to Paris that evening. From there, we'd travel to Newhaven on the train and then on the boat to Dieppe. We were short of time, and I was disappointed not to have a chance to see London and appreciate it properly. I'd read so much about different parts of London that there was a sort of magic relating to them in my mind; it was the centre of the British Empire and home to some of the biggest political figures the world had seen – never mind the likes of Sherlock Holmes and Sexton Blake. And wasn't the famous school known as Greyfriars located somewhere outside London where Harry Wharton, Bob Cherry and Billy Bunter always found themselves at loggerheads with Mr Quelch?

But because we were only just passing through I didn't even get a chance to see Speakers' Corner at Marble Arch where the 'god-creators and god-destroyers' could be heard every Sunday. I bought a copy of the *Daily Worker*. I couldn't but laugh when I saw the tip they gave for the Grand National – *Blue Shirt*! I sent the postcard home to tell them I was going to hang around London for another few days.

When we reached Victoria Station a group of men were waiting for us all of whom had the same destination as ourselves – Englishmen, Scotsmen, Welshmen,[1] and a number of Irishmen who were based in England. We were part of this group and yet we were also independent of it at the same time. Jack Nalty was in charge of our group and no one but he issued orders to us. On the train to Newhaven were a bunch of English students chatting away happily and spouting school-French. On the boat to France I tried to have a sleep but couldn't manage it; the noise of the boat's engine kept me awake. Dieppe finally and then the train to Paris and with our own carriage and all! Jack was smoking *Gauloises* now because he preferred those French cigarettes to any others, and I often saw him afterwards swapping *Players* for *Gauloises*. The others who didn't like these French cigarettes at all used to refer to them as 'Gaw Lousies'.

'What's that book you have?' Jack says to me when we'd settled ourselves in one of the train carriages. 'Volume One of *The Olive Field* by Ralph Bates', I say and he laughed. 'I've Volume Two in my pocket here', he says. But to tell you the truth, I read very little of it. I couldn't focus on the book while we were travelling. We were quiet for most of the journey staring out the windows – and in my own case daydreaming with eyes open. We reached Paris. Jim (Francis) O'Regan got lost in the crowd on the platform or outside the station somewhere and we couldn't find him for ages. But when we reached our destination in Paris who was there waiting for us but Jim. Apparently, when he'd realised that he was lost he'd bought a copy of *L'Humanité* the newspaper of the French Communist Party, then located a gendarme that showed him how to get to the address we'd to go to using bits of sign language. Strangely enough, the policeman sent him the right way too!

Similar to London we didn't have time to look around Paris properly, so I didn't get to see the Champs Elysées where, back in 1860, John Mitchel had met Myles Byrne wearing the crest of the Legion of Honour. Nor did I have a chance to see the Place de la Bastille or where the three musketeers had lived either. My head was filled with thoughts of famous people historical and legendary now that we were in Paris. They all melded as one in my imagination – D'Artagnan was as true for me as Danton was, and Billy Bunter as true as Baldwin. We had a bath, a meal and went to bed. The following day we all went for a medical.

The medicals were held in a huge room where nothing was private. There were three or four doctors in attendance to cater for the different languages being spoken and, needless to say, the doctors were multilingual themselves. They all sat at the top of the room and after taking off our clothes we walked up to see the doctor, one by one. O'Regan's friend, the second Cork-man, was rejected for duty because he was flatfooted. He was really downhearted and dejected saying goodbye to us. Another person, an Englishman was asked by a doctor whether he'd ever had rheumatic fever. 'I did,' he told them. Apparently, this disease affects the heart and the doctor had been able to tell straight away. This man was rejected for duty also. During the medical, every man had to squeeze his penis so that it could be examined more closely. One man didn't do this to the satisfaction of the doctor and the latter responded loudly – so that everyone in the room heard it: 'There's a man here who can't squeeze his penis!'

The men who passed the medical were gathered into groups and each group was given instructions in their own language in addition to a sum of money to travel to Béziers in southern France. Despite the fact that we spoke English our lads were duly recognised as an Irish military company and Jack accepted as our leader. That same day we found ourselves on the train to Béziers, a city close to the Pyrenees Mountains and one of the principal cities of the Languedoc. Our group now comprised five men in total – Jack Nalty, Paddy Duff, Jim (James Francis) O'Regan, Hughie Hunter, and me. On the train to Béziers we didn't talk a whole lot; in between bits of scattered conversation, we spent our time smoking and thinking and looking out at the landscape passing by. Jack was in the seat directly opposite mine. It was obvious that he was eager and ready to get back into battle. The way he saw it, compared to this (i.e., the war in Spain), everything else was dull and boring. Jack was on his way back to Spain as was his close friend Paddy Duff. Given that I'd no experience then of war, I didn't really understand how brave these men really were. It's easy enough for the new recruit starting out as he'd be blind to the perils of the battlefield and to the terrible injuries and wounds that people suffer. Both Jack and Paddy were more than aware of the dangers and hardships that awaited them, yet they were still keen to return to battle. They'd already witnessed their own comrades dying at Cordoba and Jarama. They hadn't been deluded by the 'magic' of war – in theory. They'd already played their part and they could've given up at that point. And yet, despite all this they'd returned. That's real and true bravery. Jack was very similar to Frank Ryan in ways. He was a strong-willed man and devoted to the cause – someone you could always rely on. Thinking such thoughts and looking out at the vineyards either side of me, we reached Béziers from where I sent another postcard home.

We made our way to a small hotel as per the instructions given to us in Paris. Jack, Paddy, Jim, and I were in the same room, a nice comfortable room with two double beds even if the bidet baffled us at first. Hughie Hunter was put in a different room. The following morning after breakfast we went out and relaxed on some benches on the boulevard and sunned ourselves. We couldn't stay too far from the hotel as we didn't know the local area at all. Because we didn't have passports it was also dangerous for us to have any contact with the police, so we were very careful not to attract the attention of the gendarmes at any stage. The food was good and so too was the light French beer. In the local café, we could see into the kitchen where the women were preparing the food, shelling the peas and the like. Between the lovely food, the French beer, and the sun, we were really enjoying life and I was in no great hurry myself to leave a place as nice as this. It wasn't long however before we got word that everything was in order for the next stage of our journey. While we'd been waiting in Béziers, other small groups of volunteers from different countries had been arriving, all of whom were scattered around different parts of the city.

Now we all joined together and journeyed by charabanc to somewhere that was at the foot of the Pyrenees where everyone congregated in a huge barn – around 50 or 60 men altogether. In addition to English, you could hear French, Italian, German and other languages I didn't recognise being spoken. The talk was excited and lively, all the different languages running into each other like a series of musical instruments. Everyone was thinking the same thing. This great event was only just beginning. Spain was only a short distance away from us now. The sound of the voices grew louder and suddenly one of the French leaders warned everyone that the noise was too loud and we needed to be quieter. By gathering together like this secretly at night, we were already breaking the law even if it was difficult to believe that the authorities didn't know what was going on. I suppose that they let on that there was nothing out of the ordinary happening. But all the same, we didn't need to attract their attention to ourselves. After a short while, when everything was ready and organised we went outside into the pitch-black night.

Our guide was very experienced. He was used to the Pyrenees and knew the mountain routes well and we followed this man one by one as we began our climb. It was so dark that you could barely see the man in front of you; I had to follow the person directly in front of me by putting my hand on his shoulder, like a game of blind man's buff. We slipped and fell often as we made the climb, the ground was so rough and uneven. And all the while, there wasn't a word from anyone. This is how we began our illegal journey climb across the Pyrenees, a line of men walking slowly and carefully, winding along like a snake and climbing higher and higher all the while. There was nothing but a very narrow path in some places. At one stage I slipped and instinctively grabbed hold of the person in front of me and we both fell to the ground. The man I'd grabbed hold of was Scottish and he cursed me in a low voice. I told him I was sorry. Afterwards I found out that the same man had spent time in the British Army and that he'd done his military training in the Black Watch or 'An Freicadan Dubh' as it was known in Scots Gaelic. 'Naturally enough,' I said to myself on hearing this. 'He's better at this than I am – walking like this in complete darkness.'

By the time we were halfway across the mountain I was fit to collapse. It never occurred to me that this was just a taster of the climbing that awaited us when we did our training in Spain itself. We continued climbing throughout the night until dawn and then suddenly we were making our descent again. After a while, we spotted a road at the bottom of the mountain, a short distance away from which stood a house on level ground. We rested here. Now that the climb was over our exhaustion had disappeared. I felt that I could do it again. I lay down on the ground and looked up at the sun slowly rising in a blue and perfect sky. A dog ran over and back barking excitedly. Eventually we spied them in the distance – the lorries arriving to pick us up. They came to a stop at the foot of the hill and we went down to them.

Off we went on the journey towards Figueras. Now that we'd had a rest everyone was in flying form again. With all the happy chatter and singing, you'd have thought we were on holidays, not going to war. There was a big German lad in the first lorry with a very powerful voice and he sang all the way to our destination – an old fortress, a short distance on the outskirts of Figueras that was under the army's control. A banner hung over the entrance gate and I remember what was written on it as clear as day – *Ejército Popular* – The People's Army. The lorries went in through the gate and, for the first time ever, I saw the Republican flag fluttering high over the centre of the yard – red, yellow, and purple. We were on Spanish soil at last. We were given a meal and then we all went to sleep.

Next morning, following breakfast, we gathered in the yard and saluted the flag and it was raised high. This was our first duty every morning because this flag was much more than a piece of cloth stuck to a pole. It was a symbol of the people's hungry desire for freedom.

We undertook our second duty then – while we were drilling in the fields outside – which was to learn the different military orders and instructions in Spanish so that we could recognise them all immediately. Learning like this meant that we got an interesting insight into how to teach a language without wasting time on textbooks, blackboards, grammatical problems, and other similar ridiculous and stupid methods. It was amazing how quickly we learned Spanish – or as much of it as we needed anyway. I was given an opportunity to be in charge of the group and without boasting about it I think I was very good at giving orders to other people and making them sweat while I stood there shouting my instructions. 'POR LA CABEZA – ADELANTE! (BY THE HEAD – FORWARD)' This was the favourite order that every man wanted to hear when the heat was killing him. 'EN SU LUGAR – DESCANSO! (IN PLACE – REST – AT EASE!)'

One day, Jack Nalty was delighted to run into a man in the office he knew from when he'd been injured previously at Cordoba in December 1936. This man had been injured in the same battle as he had and each of them had been assigned to an office job afterwards. A short while later and Jack and Paddy both had to return to the brigade ranks.

'So long', says Jack in that way of his.

'Hasta la vista', says I, trying out my Spanish.

There was a large hut in the yard where about ten prisoners were being held. These were *Internacionales* who'd been imprisoned for various misdemeanors. One day I was ordered to guard the prisoners. On the other side of the yard, directly opposite the hut, was the toilet. Whenever a prisoner indicated that he wanted to go to the toilet, the guard had to let him out and re-lock the door of the hut behind him, then accompany the prisoner to the toilet and back again. The prisoners were lying on the ground which was covered with loose hay. I could talk to them through the door. One of them, an American, told me that they were to be executed. I gave him some cigarettes at one stage. I didn't enjoy this guard duty much. I spoke to an officer later about this and he laughed.

'They all say that they're sentenced to death. And then they get cigarettes for free from the softies.' I said nothing in response to this. A short while later I was put on night-duty as a sentry. I had to swap with guards on the main gate twice during the night. That Scotsman whom I mentioned earlier, the man who'd received his training in the Black Watch – I'd have to wake him up at 2 or 3 o'clock in the morning.

'It's your turn now,' says I, 'and I hope its black enough for you.'

'Are you looking for promotion already?' he says, getting up and joining me outside. To tell you the truth, you didn't need any guards in this place; it was so far away from the fighting. Our rifles weren't even loaded. Discipline and training, that's what this was about.

After we'd been there for a while, we'd to do another medical. The reason for this apparently was to see whether the journey across the Pyrenees had affected any of us and whether any of us had any weakness or medical problem that the doctors in Paris had failed to diagnose. Strangely enough, one young man was discovered to have a ruptured hernia and he was sent home. God knows how he'd even managed to disguise such an injury while he was in Paris.

I was unloading bags of flour when I was suddenly called to go for my medical. I went straight over to where the doctor was examining everyone and walked straight into the room to him.

'Why's your heartbeat so fast?' the doctor asks me.

'I was lifting and carrying bags of flour and I'm not used to that kind of work,' says I.

'Sit down there for a minute, he says, and he went on examining some others. I stayed where I was for a while, worried in case there was something wrong, but the heartbeat had slowed down by the time he came back to me, and I was free to go.

We continued with our drilling and practicing. When marching, the Spaniards had a habit of swinging their arms across in front of their chests instead of keeping them straight by their sides. And we knew all the Spanish orders by heart at this stage. Most of us were new recruits who'd never had any training before. But there was the odd person there – like the man from the Black Watch who'd served in the British Army. An Englishman by the name of Bonfield[2] told me that his family had strong links with the army, and that he himself had even been born in an army barracks. In fairness, you couldn't really beat that for a good start in this line of business. Another Englishman I was chatting to one day while on sentry duty sitting on a chair outside the front gate told me that he'd worked as a guard outside Buckingham Palace for a number of years. The Queen would ask the King: 'Who's on guard-duty tonight?' When the King told her that it was your man, this put her mind at rest: 'I'll sleep sound tonight', she'd say.

It was little stories like this that passed the time for us at night. One morning I spotted the prisoners leaving to do some vital work as part of a work-squad, as someone informed me. I was delighted to see them leaving. I felt as if there was some dark cloud over the place whenever they were there, locked in the hut all day. We received our pay for the first time –ten pesetas a day, paid once a month. It was in paper money; coins weren't used in the Republic. Each local authority issued their own money which could be spent only within the boundaries of their own areas or towns. Go outside that area, and the money was worthless. No sooner had we been paid, but we were told that we were leaving this barracks and a collection was immediately taken up for *El Socorro Rojo Internacional* (International Red Aid). We thought the timing of this collection was very funny altogether.

CHAPTER 3

BARCELONA

'Better to die on your feet than live on your knees'

We left Figueras and headed for Barcelona. On leaving, little did we realise that it would be in this province of Ampurdán and its principal town Figueras that the Cortes would come together for the last time in February 1939, the city crowded with people trying to escape Franco's soldiers who were hot on their heels and their bomber planes causing destruction all around. The war would be nearly over by then with Franco assuming control of Catalonia. This sad day had yet to arrive. We reached Barcelona only to find everything in chaos around us.

On 9 March 1938, Franco initiated a ferocious assault in Aragon and the Republican Army had to retreat. A lot of territory was lost, and Franco took control of Gandesa and captured more than 100 men from the 15th International Brigade. Franco reached the Mediterranean on 15 April, Good Friday. It was an appropriate date from the Republican perspective. The Republic had been cut in two. Worse still, the few weeks prior to this had seen 17 air raids on the city lasting for two days. 1,300 people were killed and 2,000 injured. The Italian planes came in from Mallorca, a short distance from Barcelona. They normally cut their engines just before reaching the city, gliding in silently on arrival. The German Ambassador himself used the word 'terrible' to refer to this massacre. Juan Negrín, the Prime Minister of the Republic spoke as follows: 'Resistir significa vencer. Resistir con pan o sin pan, con ropa, o sin ropa, con fusiles o sin ellos, no pasarán.' ('To resist means to win. To resist with bread or without bread, with clothes or without clothes, with rifles or without rifles, they won't get through.') These words echoed the exhortation that La Pasionaria had given earlier in the war: 'Mas vale morir de pie que vivir de rodillas.' ('Better to die on your feet than live on your knees.') Or: 'Death rather than oppression.' No wonder Churchill rallied the British people during the Second World War by asking them to imitate 'the brave men of Barcelona.'

Next, Tortosa was captured by the Italians supporting Franco. For the first time the war was on Catalan soil. The city officials weren't sure what was going on at the battlefront. We met men who'd been separated from their military units and were trying to find out what they should do next.

I was in an office one day with a group of random soldiers when Pat Murphy, a sailor from Cardiff was introduced to me. 'We got a right hammering at the Ebro,' he said. 'We think that Frank Ryan was captured but we're not sure!' While the barracks was being prepared for us, we stayed in a building somewhere and slept on the floor. One night before returning to the room where we slept, I drank a few glasses of red wine (wine was 50 centimos or half-a-peseta a glass). I slept very soundly on the floor that night. The following morning, when I got up, the Scotsman asked me: 'What did you make of the air-raid last night?' 'What air-raid?', I said. They'd attacked the docks during the night, but I'd never heard a sound. Good on you, wine!

Eventually we were garrisoned in the Karl Marx Barracks. This place was also close to the docks. In the barracks yard you could buy muscatel, vermouth, and absinthe. In the sleeping quarters, someone had hung a rubber Johnny on the back of the door. No one paid any heed to it except for the English-speakers who made jokes about it in half-embarrassed tones. There were no seats on the toilets; you'd to crouch on your hunkers and they claimed that this was a healthier way of going to the toilet. There was a strong smell of your urine everywhere. We didn't do any training – all we had to do was 'pass the time' somehow. In the Barracks yard one day I was chatting to Bill Bibby[1] from Liverpool. A young man, he was tall, dark, and handsome and sported a small moustache. The Spaniards were used to American actors visiting their country. One time, a Spanish soldier walked up to us and pointed in Bill's direction.

'Clark Gable?', he says to me.

I shook my head. 'Inglés', says I, and he was very disappointed. No doubt about it, but Bill looked very like the film star alright. Bill made the most of his chances too. One day we were in Woolworths and even though he had very little Spanish he managed to make a date with a girl who was one of the shop assistants. He had a problem however – no money. He got around it though. On leaving England he'd brought a strong pair of new shoes with him and now he decided to sell them. That afternoon Bill and I left the barracks and went up to the long, wide avenue known as Las Ramblas. A passage for strollers ran down through the centre of the avenue and all types of sellers and stalls were set up there. The most common things available there included newspapers, magazines, books, flowers, and the like. There were shoeshine boys and cobblers in amongst all these dealers and hawkers also. It was a mortal sin at the time apparently to wear unpolished shoes. And if you needed rubber soles on your shoes, they could do them right there and then for you. We spotted one of these cobblers and went over to him. Bill held out the new shoes to him. They were a brown gold colour and beautifully polished. And now, with the sun gleaming on them they looked incredible.

'Cuántos pesetas', says Bill, 'you give me...?', but the man cut across him.

'Ah si, comprendo', says the man. He took the shoes from Bill, put one of them up on the awl and began fixing a rubber-sole to it.

'No, no', says Bill, gesticulating.

'Cuántos pesetas you give me for the shoes?', but he continued with his work tacking the sole to the bottom of the shoe, saying, 'comprendo bien camarada.'

Following a whole heap of funny hand movements and sign language Bill managed to indicate what he wanted, and they made a deal. How he managed to attract that girl with such limited Spanish I'll never know. Maybe she really thought he was Clark Gable after all!

If you wanted to relax in the seat in the Ramblas in those days, it cost you ten centimos or one-tenth of a peseta. One day a group of us were drinking coffee in a café there when the waiter heard that we were recruits for the International Brigade. The young man took a gun from beneath the counter and demonstrated it to us rather melodramatically. It was clear that people who weren't official members of the armed forces, were still ready to defend the Republic against the enemy within – 'the fifth column' as they referred to them. I don't remember hearing any newspaper-sellers on the streets of Barcelona the way you'd have heard them in Dublin back then. 'Herrolormail' (*Herald* or *Mail*) or '*Stop Press! Terrible Discovery Found Out!*'

In the Parque de Ciudadela (City Park), which also contained the animal gardens, we met an American who was happy to decline all the irregular verbs in Spanish for us – all for the price of a few cigarettes: another wandering soldier lost in Spain! We were relaxing in the park and sunning ourselves and 'Happy' Cunningham,[2] a Scotsman was singing to his heart's content. He was a very sweet singer. He could sing a song that you'd heard a thousand times before, but you'd have sworn you were hearing it sung properly for the very first time. Another young man who had a fine voice was Frank Airlie from Newcastle[3] in the north of England. Only Jim O'Regan from Cork could compare with him on the singing front, and his favourite song was 'Kelly the Boy from Killane'.

We spent a lovely afternoon relaxing in that park. The section of the Ramblas that we frequented most ran up from the Cristobal Colón to the Plaza de Cataluña, and we explored the narrow winding streets that skirted both sides of the Ramblas as well. Down here, you couldn't help but notice how the iron balconies on many houses had been twisted out of shape because of the bombing. On one of these streets was a small cinema showing the famous film *Battleship Potemkin*. I saw the film there for the first time in the company of Jim O'Regan. This was one of the Soviet films that Russian ambassador Marcel Rosenberg brought into Spain with him. They were difficult and hungry times. We got garbanzos (chickpeas in English) to eat, and I liked them a lot. Some of the other men couldn't stand them but I couldn't get enough of them. The fact that we were eating in the Ritz – because that's the hotel where we were staying – you might have been expecting posher food than peas!

Once, we were eating food in a basement somewhere and hungry children were on the path outside, begging for food, their thin hands stretching in through the grates of the basement. Ice cream, coffee, and wine; these were three things you could spend your money on in those days. On my own one day, I visited the animal gardens in the Parque de Ciudadela. The entrance fee was 50 centimos, the same price as a glass of vino tinto. There wasn't much to see in there that day – just a few small sad animals. I suppose it was probably too dangerous for them to keep animals such as lions and tigers while the war was going on. I saw a glass case full of bees working diligently on a honeycomb; they were the liveliest animals I saw in the gardens that day. I left the park and turned right and found myself in Calle de Wellington – another Dubliner one might say. I thought of Phoenix Park and the Wellington Monument back home where I'd often played as a schoolboy. Back on the main street I drank a glass of wine in honour of the occasion.

I didn't see any sentry on-duty at the barracks. Apparently, soldiers and others could come and go as they pleased. Every morning a chatty low-sized man would arrive. I don't know where he was from or even what his name was. He wasn't in the army and I don't know how he earned his living, but he had excellent English. He arrived one day, having sorted out some dispute or other in his workplace, he said: 'Thank God I decided to learn English.' This man had a habit of producing a mouth organ all of a sudden from his pocket and playing a quick tune. One morning after he'd called in, himself, myself, and Hughie Hunter from Belfast took a walk from the barracks down to the bay. When we reached where the Cristobal Colón is, the man began to recount the days when the army had risen up against the government in July 1936, and what happened in Barcelona at that juncture. Apparently, the army had planned to take over the city-centre – the Plaza de Cataluña – and then spread outwards from there to assume control of the entire city. Early that morning on the Sunday, the 19 July, the soldiers (around 10,000 of them) left the various barracks throughout the city to put this plan into effect. But the people of Barcelona were ready for them. They came out onto the streets in their thousands to challenge the military who found barricades everywhere impeding their progress. Ferocious street battles took place in Plaza de le Universidad, Plaza de España, El Paralelo, Plaza de Cataluña, Paseo de Colón, las Atarazanas, and other places throughout the city. In the Plaza de Cataluña the military took over La Telefónica, a tall building that was the nerve-centre for the whole Plaza. The workers and the mounted police attacked the military relentlessly until hundreds of dead bodies covered the entire square, all gunned down by machine guns. The people suffered terrible losses before finally emerging victorious. The ferocious way that the people launched themselves at them and the way that they died as if without a care had horrified the military and come as a real shock to them. They'd expected an easy victory and never imagined encountering courage and stubborn resistance of such magnitude.

Close to the bay, in the Paseo de Colón, stood the building known as the La Capitanía. General Manuel Goded from Mallorca had flown in to lead the rebels and it was there that he'd had his headquarters. He'd been forced to surrender later in the day however, about 7 o'clock that evening. The last place to surrender to the crowd was Las Atarazanas, a big, fortified barracks close to Cristobal Colón. More people died there than anywhere else. The soldiers didn't surrender until the following day, on the Monday morning. Because the various companies hadn't managed to unite together as one, they were beaten at different locations as they were separated from one another, and it was only after enormous bloodshed that the military rising was put down in Barcelona.

On the way over to Spain we hadn't had enough time to research the history of the different places we now found ourselves in. Now, finally we had that chance – even if time was still fairly limited – to explore the city and take in some of its history. The events I've just recounted were still fresh in the memory as they'd taken place there so recently – and yet they were also already a part of history. Every plaza, calle, edificio – and nearly every rock and stone – had its own living, breathing history associated with it. And this man who was our guide knew it all. He showed us the exact spot in the Calle Santa Madrona where Francisco Ascaso of the CNT (Anarchist Trade Union Federation) had fallen in the battle against Las Atarazanas. A wreath of flowers, red and black – the Anarchist colours – had been laid on the spot, and remained there for weeks. After the fighting he said the city had to gather up all the dead horses from the various barracks and streets, and the putrid smell of the dead animals was so strong that the city workers had to wear protective masks over their noses and eyes. We went up Las Ramblas to La Plaza de Cataluña and the small man took a sharp turn to the right. 'I'll show you the place where Catalan independence was publicly declared in 1931 and where an end was put to the monarchy.' We went up the Calle Fernando until we reached Plaza San Jaime. In this square stood two fine buildings directly opposite one another, La Casa de la Ciudad (City Hall) and the *Generalidad* where the offices of the Catalan Government were located.

On 14 April 1931, Lluis Companys[4] raised the Republican flag – red, yellow and purple – over the balcony of City Hall and spoke to the small crowd gathered there. A short while later Frances Macià emerged onto the balcony of the *Generalidad* to a square that was crowded with people by then, and proclaimed Catalan independence in the language of the Catalan people. I took in all these buildings with great reverence and respect. In my mind's eye, I saw Pearse reading the Easter Proclamation beneath the columns of the GPO. Then it was back to Las Ramblas.

Your man showed us the hill Montjuich – the Hill of the Jews – which was to the right as you looked down over the bay. It was within the fortress there that General Goded was executed for being a traitor to the Republic. All of a sudden our guide said goodbye to us, produced the mouth organ from his pocket, and off he went playing quietly to himself.

CHAPTER 4

THROUGH CATALONIA

The evening eventually arrived when we left the city behind us – the blue lamps, the plane trees on the Ramblas, the noise of the trams with their elderly conductors, the pigeons in the Plaza de Cataluña and Karl Marx Barracks. Then began our constant journeying from place to place throughout Catalonia before we eventually reached the British Battalion – then preparing for the battle that lay ahead at the Ebro. During the course of our odyssey throughout Catalonia, we spent a short while in Olot, a small industrial or market town about 30 miles from Figueras. This was the main city for the region of La Garrotxa in north-east Catalonia. We found lodgings in the Collegio de Olot y Convento de Padres Carmelitas. After the revolt was put down in Barcelona the Padres had been scattered (they'd been scattered to other areas by the order of 'del Gobierno de la Generalidad de Cataluña') as enforced by the 'Federacio Local de Syndicates Unios d'Olot' on the 22 July 1936 and, for a while afterwards, this building has been used as a barracks for the *milicianos*.

On arriving here, we were gathered together in the yard when I noticed another group there before us whose officer-in-charge was in a bit of trouble. A group of soldiers had gathered around him, insulting and cursing him. One of them was angrily calling out in broken Spanish – 'mucho comida para oficiales – para nosotros nada.'('Plenty of food for the officers, but for us nothing'). The officer in question just stood there quietly before them in dignified fashion without saying a word. Someone told me that he was American. I'm not sure what was the nationality of the soldiers that were complaining.

We stayed here for just a few days and we had small rooms similar to cells for sleeping in. Our first night there, the thought struck me – 'The Padres or (perhaps) student-clerics who'd been meditating and contemplating the mysteries of the Faith, where were they all now?' There were various messages written on the walls but, it was clear from a political perspective that whoever had written them, it certainly wasn't the Padres anyway! On the following morning a group of us emerged from a café close to the collegio to see lorries full of new recruits arriving in our direction from Plaza Clará. And who jumped down from one of the lorries but Bill McGregor from Inchicore, Dublin! I was amazed to see Bill there above anyone else because when I'd left Dublin he'd been in Russia studying at the Lenin School. I was sure that the Party [Communist Party of Ireland] wouldn't have given him permission to come to Spain. They didn't have that many educated members to spare. Sure enough – as he explained it to me right there and then – the Party had been strongly against him coming to Spain but he'd refused to give into them on this question. He was very keen on coming to Spain and that was the end of it. He laughed at the puttees I was wearing. I hated them myself. I didn't like the look of them or the amount of time it took to put them on properly. And another reason I didn't like them was that they reminded me of the British soldiers in Dublin when I was young. I was delighted when eventually I managed to get rid of them.

Bill McGregor (Dublin) at the Lenin School Moscow, 1937

In Olot, I got to know 'Comrade Brown,' an Englishman. He was a very sophisticated man and very confident in himself. On the first day that Brown, 'Happy' Cunningham (a Scotsman) and I were walking around the town, feeling hungry as usual, Brown suddenly blurted out – 'Follow me!' He went into a café and 'café' was the right name for this place too – because there was nothing else to be had there except coffee – at this juncture. 'Sit down at the table there', he said. He went up to the counter to speak to the owner. Next thing, we heard the owner of the café say animatedly. 'No hay, no hay!' (There's nothing.) But Brown continued speaking to him quietly in a low voice. All of a sudden, the man disappeared into the back of the shop, into the kitchen. We couldn't believe it a short while afterwards when big plates of fried eggs were placed in front of the three of us. Brown never revealed what he'd said to the owner for him to produce this miracle for us. I don't remember that he paid for the food either. This was just another of the big unsolved mysteries of the Spanish Civil War!

The next day we moved to a small village about a mile or so outside Olot. It was obvious that no preparations had been made beforehand for our arrival. There was nowhere for us to sleep so we had to bed down in the local church that was around the corner at the top of the street. The church was completely bare and empty. There weren't any benches, even inside it. And there was just the one street running through this village surrounded by fields. We were allowed to gather loose hay in the fields which we spread on the floor of the church for lying on, come evening. Just as we were getting ready to bed down for the night, a group of girls ran in to the church and for a joke, they starting tugging on the bell-rope and ringing the bell that hung down near the side of the altar. I thought I was an out-and-out atheist but I have to admit that this incident disturbed me. There I was standing in the middle of a bare church up to my knees in hay staring at these girls who were just skitting and having the craic. To me it demonstrated the distinction between the anti-clericalism of the Irish person – someone who could still be a good Catholic at the same time – and the basic antipathy that the lower classes in Spain exhibited towards the church. It was based on their own personal experience that this hostile attitude had emerged. There is no denying that the fault for this lay with the church itself and that the clergy paid dearly for their neglect of the Spanish public. The way the ordinary people saw it, the church was just a protective shield for the monied class. There is an old saying in Spanish that goes: 'Dios es omnipotente, y el dinero es su teniente' ('God is omnipotent but money operates as his secretary.') I've never heard a similar phrase in the Irish language. In a strange way, there was a religious strain running through this Spanish anti-clericalism. Buenaventura Durruti, the famous leader of the *Federación Anarquista Ibérica* (the Iberian Anarchist Federation) spoke at a public gathering in the Plaza Cataluña in Barcelona in August 1936. As part of his speech that day, he said: 'I swear to you that I won't be satisfied until every church in Spain is burned to the ground and the power of the church completely destroyed. I swear this to you on my solemn oath in the name of the Father and the Son, and the Holy Spirit.'

I remember that I had no spoon the first time that we had food in this new place. We were gathered together in this big empty room that had no benches or chairs. The Scotsman, 'Sailor,' as he was known – because he always wore a sailor's cap – had put his food down on the table but had turned aside to have a chat with someone and I swiped his spoon and began eating. Needless to say, I planned on leaving it back in his food before he stopped chatting or noticed. I was only just borrowing it for a minute. He finished his chat before I'd realised and before I could say anything. When he spotted that his spoon was missing what did he do but let a roar out of him and run out the door! I continued eating away and he came back next minute with a big smile on his face and a different spoon in his hand. One of the locals must have given it to him, I suppose. Seeing as he was happy again and I didn't want to cause any trouble, I said nothing about swiping his spoon in the first place. That was how I managed to get my hands on a replacement for the one I'd lost myself.

I was walking down the street one morning when I passed a stable door on my right hand side. The door was open and out of curiosity I looked in and spotted three middle-aged Englishmen sitting on the floor. They were drinking wine from a basin they'd placed in the middle of the stable floor. Each man had a mug in his hands and they were filling it with a ladle. They invited me in and I took a drink from the ladle. After a while I left the stables because it was lunchtime and the other three men went on drinking. Later that day, outside the church, I spotted some men carrying one of the drinkers into a small stone house where they locked him in a shed there. The following morning as I passed by the house, I spotted the same man looking out through the window, a sad look on his face. I don't know how those men had managed to get their hands on all that wine or who'd paid for it – or if anyone had paid for it even.

After a short while staying in the abandoned church, we divided up and moved into different houses in the village. These houses were owned by rich people but they'd left the area. In the house, I met a young Englishman by the name of Johnny Longstaff [1] and we discovered a collection of coins. We went down to the wine shop and it's no exaggeration to say that 'the landlady's eyes opened wide with delight'[2] when she saw the coins – because there was only paper money to be had there at the time! We bought plenty of wine that day, I can tell you!

Now that we were billeted in various houses, a Spanish officer would regularly inspect the rooms. Any complaints he had were translated for us by Manuel. Manuel was a lively young Latin-American lad who spoke fluent Spanish. At night he could be seen in the local pubs singing and all the girls gathered around him: 'Yo te quiero mucho, mucho mucho' (a pop-song that was common then, I suppose.) We played a soccer match one day, the Spaniards against the English-speakers. The Spaniards won but I had a good excuse. I was a Gaelic footballer, not a soccer player.

Myself and Bill McGregor spotted a house at the top of a hill one day and we thought that there might be food of some type to be bought there and so we walked up to the top of the hill and knocked on the door. The man of the house let us in. A woman sat in front of an empty table, a child in her lap. There was hardly anything in the house except for the two chairs and the table in the middle of the room. The place looked poor. The couple looked over at us with downcast expressions and we showed them some money.

'Do you have any eggs?' They didn't.

'Do you have bread?' They didn't.

We gave the man a few cigarettes and left.

A Spanish officer came to speak to us one day. We all gathered around him and he gave us an enthusiastic and rousing speech. For some reason however, Manuel wasn't around to translate the speech into English. From what I could tell, the officer's main point – even if I didn't understand everything he said – was that no sacrifice, no matter how great, was too much if we really wished to achieve our objectives. The man described quite realistically the hardship of war and the terrible injuries and wounds some of us would have to suffer if we were to win the war.

'No hay nada tan terrible como una guerra civil.' ('There is no war as terrible as a civil war.') Short simple sentences such as this in Spanish, I still remember them to this very day. He said the last sentence of his speech slowly but with great emphasis and passion, a lump in his throat. 'La lucha es dura–pero es magnifica!' ('The struggle is hard but it is a glorious one!') Even the men who couldn't understand Spanish felt the intense passion and power of his speech and were really affected by it. There was no need of a translation, in all honesty. The spin and propaganda that insults the mind, there was no trace of it from this man's mouth. Every word he said was harsh and bitter truth. Everything he said and the way he said it was all the more inspiring and powerful as a consequence.

One of the Englishmen amongst us got the loan of a bicycle one day from a girl in the village so as to go to Olot. While he was there, however, the bike was stolen. For whatever reason he was reluctant to go back to the girl and tell her what had happened. This man wore a peaked cap. He was one of the few as most of the men wore a beret or a woollen cap. The following morning we were leaving this latest place and for fear that this girl and her mother might spot us leaving the man swapped his hat with another man who wore a beret. With the beret on, they never recognised him! I couldn't understand why he didn't just tell the girl straight out what had happened. I myself had left my watch into a shop to be repaired and I left Olot without it.

The Spaniards were very good at drinking from bottles made of pigskin. They raised the pigskin up over their heads and the wine or water would fall straight into their mouths. I tried to imitate them a couple of times but I had to give up in the end. Most of the drink would have ended up on the ground otherwise.

Sometimes it seemed to me that we were travelling aimlessly through the whole of Catalonia. This was a consequence of the confusion and lack of organisation following the defeat in Aragon, I suppose. But it is important to say that the authorities had to get over much bigger problems than worrying about us or the situation we Brigade members now found ourselves in. I don't remember the names of half of the places we passed through, even if certain places and incidents still come back to me now that I am older.

In one place, I saw a man threshing corn in the ancient way. He was standing in the middle of a circle leading a horse by rope that walked around and around, trampling down the corn. The man's horse was his threshing machine. It was easy to see how hard these farm labourers' lives were, given that they were still reliant on such old-fashioned agricultural methods. We only saw oranges in one place. We passed a lorry on the side of the road somewhere full of oranges for export, as we were told. 'Red oranges,' I'm sure! (There are many Arab words in the Spanish language and one of them is this word for orange i.e. *naranja.)*

Where was I one day when I saw horses whinnying and frothing at the bit as they pawed the earth? Next to the horses stood a group of horsemen sheltering in the shade of the trees, chatting with one another and laughing. Where was I one day when I spotted some young soldiers sitting on the ground, books in their hands and someone teaching them how to read? Or the sight of the women of the village washing clothes at the communal bath? Based on the phrases scrawled on many of the walls we passed, it was clear that the anarchist philosophy was very strong in Catalonia.

One morning we stood outside a cemetery's walls and fired a volley of shots into the air above it. I can't remember who was buried there or what he'd done to deserve this honour; unfortunately, given how many years have passed, I can't even remember the name of the place where we fired this volley of shots at this stage. In one small village, an Englishman named Bruce Boswell[3] performed a scene from the American play, *Waiting for Lefty*. Boswell was involved with the Unity Theatre in London and very experienced in stagecraft.

Passing through in the countryside, we saw the many olive gardens and the groves growing almonds and lemons… And yet in the cities, the train stations were full of children begging…Most nights, we slept outside beneath the sky, a short distance from some village or other; I slept beneath more empty olive trees than ones in full bloom! We regularly found ourselves sleeping out in the open staring up at the stars arguing, debating, laughing and telling stories before finally falling asleep beneath the trees. One night in an olive grove somewhere, it occurred to me that there was no lack of 'olive branches' in that country, this despite the war exploding all around us. Catalonia was very like Connemara in places, hilly, craggy, and with a terrain that was wild and rough. Maybe it was just my imagination but I also thought that the Catalan people were similar to Connemara people in places. Listening to the lively conversation of the locals in Catalonia – even if I understood very little of what was being said, just the odd word maybe – reminded me of the time I'd spent in Baile na hAbhann[4] in Connemara, when I was schoolboy. The Irish of the schoolbooks and the Spanish of the schoolbooks – neither are much help when you are listening to native speakers talking quickly. However, there are still advantages to be gained from literature and book-learning. A few times, when amongst the Spaniards, a nice literary sentence or phrase would come to my lips and I'd surprise them. When you're listening to someone who only has broken-English speaking – you rarely expect to hear phrases such as – 'how sweet the moonlight sleeps upon this bank' – coming from them. And yet it is very easy to learn a sentence like this off-by-heart from a book– even if the same person mightn't be able to ask for a glass of water!

In Catalonia, they have their own native language, of course – Catalan, a language that was given full, official recognition under the auspices of the Republic. In 1931, Alfonso XIII visited Barcelona and someone spoke to him in Catalan. The King indicated that he understood what the person had said to him but that he couldn't speak the language. He vowed to the man to have fluent Catalan the next time he visited Catalonia. As it happens, the Republic was set up that same year and the King was forced to flee!

Some people claim that we have no need for more than one language – that language is just a means of communication. I don't agree with this view. Every language has its own particular richness and the culture of the world is poorer for every language that dies out as a consequence. When I was young I heard a story about Goodbody's of Dublin. It mightn't be true but then again it might be too. They put a new cigar out on the market but there was no demand at all for it. Next thing, they called the brand Buenos Cuerpos and it sold well. Even when it comes to its role as a means of communication, no two languages are the same. When Franco took over the Basque Country in June 1937, the Bill promulgating self-rule was rescinded and the use of Basque in public was banned. The people of Catalonia knew what to expect from that man therefore.

One day myself and some other Brigade members spent the afternoon having the craic swimming in a water pool. That afternoon reminded me of a piece I'd read years earlier in a book by Brigadier General Crozier – I think it was – about the First World War. Once, during a short break he was watching some soldiers swimming and the thought ran through his mind: How many of these young strong healthy men will be dead and gone before long? Now and again, such negative thoughts would come into our minds also. That same night we found ourselves at the top of a hill where a man played guitar and a crowd of Spaniards all sang songs together. I leaned my back against a rock and looked down the length of that dark glen and then across at the giant grey mountains opposite us. That sad Spanish music and the sad and poignant singing in the moonlit night, full of mystery – a heavy gloom or dejection came over me and I sensed a cold harsh wind blowing through my soul. I felt a sense of despair or hopelessness coming on. It happened to me the odd time – this 'noche oscura del alma'('dark night of the soul').

After wandering through the countryside for some time we reached Cervera [Lleida Province], about a hundred miles from Barcelona. Paddy O'Sullivan from Dublin and his friend Manuel were in charge of us and this was the end of the 'easy life' we'd been having prior to this. We were left under no illusions that we were now under the strict discipline of an army and that it was our duty to salute every officer when we met them. Every morning we were marched to a certain field about a half-a-mile from the town where we performed a range of drills. Paddy kept tight control over us as a group and everyone respected him for it.

I can still remember well the incident that really alerted me to Paddy's strength of authority for the first time. We were somewhere between Olot and Cervera with a good number of strangers amongst us, the detritus of other battles, I suppose. Authority or control didn't suit them. The people in charge were trying to keep them in line for food one day but they weren't getting anywhere. Things got a bit out of control. Suddenly a young man arrived on the scene and the atmosphere changed completely. He ordered the men into line and spoke with great authority. Everyone recognised straight away that this was someone you couldn't help but take note of. They didn't cause any more trouble from then on. That man was Paddy O'Sullivan.

It was in this place Cervera that Paddy made sure we understood what was required of us as fighting men. 'I'd imagine,' he says, 'that most of you probably were involved with some political organisation or other before you came here first. Then you understand the meaning of order and discipline and the reasons for them.' Paddy put a huge emphasis on control and discipline and emphasised it again and again. He hated laxity and sloppy behaviour.

The building we were staying in now – La Universidad de Cervera – was founded by Philip X in the early eighteenth century. In 1714, all the universities in Catalonia were closed down and La Universidad de Cervera was founded to strengthen the influence of Castile in that entire region. By the nineteenth century the University's Oath of Allegiance to the Crown began as follows: 'Lejos de nosotros la funesta mania de pensar.' ('May the deadly insanity of thought remain far away from us.'). The University's columns, cloisters and ancient arches would have put you in mind of the silent meditation of the monks rather than any military setting. It was an unusual place to hear the sound of soldiers and their heavy marching feet.

One morning, out in the square, we had our breakfast eaten but there was still some food left over. We immediately formed a line to get 'seconds'. But Paddy put a stop to this plan of ours. 'There are no "seconds" for us,' he says. A group of men were on the other side of the yard waiting patiently, empty tin containers in hand. Another lorry was due in but had yet to arrive. Paddy pointed over to the other line. 'Those men there haven't had any food at all yet. We've to give them whatever's left over.' What arrangements were made with the authorities, I'm not sure – but every morning on leaving the barracks, a Spanish officer would appear and march up to the front of the company. He was a kind of a gigolo and he had a habit of waving to the señoritas who were out on the balconies watching as we passed through the streets and himself out in front 'leading the men.' Marching through those narrow, winding streets made of flagstone, he'd remove his peaked cap, smooth down his black, carefully-oiled hair and straighten his jacket. And all the while he'd be laughing quietly to himself. Once we were outside the town he'd leave us again and return the way he'd come – back to comfort some of the señoritas maybe! Once our training and drilling was finished he'd come out to meet us on the road again and we'd all walk back into town again the same way as before – with him at the front.

One day we were on our way back into town, with this officer, as usual, leading us from the front of the line, when we found ourselves hemmed in by two lorries that were blocking the road. A heated argument had erupted between two lorry drivers and we'd no choice but to come to a halt. The drivers glanced over in our direction momentarily, then returned to their argument as if we weren't even there. The Spanish officer was quite happy to stand there, a ridiculous smirk on his face, enjoying the whole performance as the two men insulted and cursed one another. The Republican Army were just spectators on this occasion! Paddy was directly behind this Spanish officer however and it was obvious that he was losing his patience with the whole spectacle. Rather than intervene and show his annoyance at the delay, it was obvious that Paddy was trying his best to control himself and keep his annoyance under wraps. He stared over impatiently at the Spaniard waiting for 'the man in charge' to intervene. But the way the Spaniard saw it, this was all just a piece of fun. Suddenly, his anger got the better of him and Paddy marched to the front – 'Venga! Venga!' he shouted loudly. The two drivers got such a fright that they jumped back into their lorries and they were gone within seconds. Paddy wasn't going to wait till mañana! The Spanish officer gave him a filthy look as much as to say 'You've just ruined all our fun now.' Then he pulled his jacket straight and with a haughty wave of his head, as a woman might do, we continued on our journey.

The next camp we reached after Cervera was a place called Vilaseca – a town situated between Falset and Tarragona, about 25 miles from the River Ebro. Gradually we were getting closer to the river where Franco's forces sat on one side and government forces on the other. A half-a-mile or so outside this town was our new training camp. There is good reason for me not to forget the name of this town – Vilaseca. In Spanish, this means 'dry town.' And yet I never witnessed Spanish rain as heavy as the rain that fell one day in this very place! When the rain started lashing down, we weren't far from a mountain cabin. Naturally enough, we made for this cabin and crowded in. A German owned this cabin as it turned out, and he got very angry with us. He began shouting and screaming and gesticulating in our direction, but no-one paid any heed to him. He was a big man. Suddenly he directed all his ire at 'Happy' Cunningham the Scotsman, for some reason. 'Happy' just laughed and said: 'Why are you attacking me – because I'm a small fella, is it?' We all thought this was hilarious. The German stopped giving out after that.

On our first day in Vilaseca I spotted a man stretched out on the ground at the side of the hill reading a book. Someone said to me, 'That's Pollock, the American; he's a Trotskyist.' The Trotskyists had their own views of the war and the best way to win it but their objectives didn't tally with the policies of the government. El Partido Obrero de Unificación Marxista (POUM) (The Workers' Party of Marxist Unification), a party that had been outlawed at this point, said that the El Partido Communista de España (PCE, Communist Party of Spain) had rejected the socialist revolution in order to appear more acceptable to the middle-classso that they might gain the support of other democratic countries. They didn't succeed in this effort however. The philosophy that the POUM had was that the working class should be put into positions of authority in the cities – and the same with farm labourers in rural areas – in order for the socialist revolution to be implemented in its entirety. They weren't really followers of Trotsky but that was the name they'd been given. The PCE placed a strong emphasis on uniting against fascism and on the urgent necessity to defend the democratic republic. For this reason, they supported the government. This was the basis for the differences that existed between the government's forces and the POUM. Each group had its own different perspective on the raison d'etre for revolution ('dos conceptos de revolución'), two perspectives that were completely at odds with one another. In order to progress their views on the revolution, both sides needed to come to some resolution or acceptance of one another's differing perspectives. I have to admit that I didn't understand this issue correctly at the time. At the juncture, I accepted the official propaganda version then espoused i.e. that the POUM were treacherously working on Franco's side and that they were just a fascist group working beneath a revolutionary image or façade. One night Paddy O'Sullivan called myself and O'Regan out on patrol with him. There were sentries on the road to make sure that no one strayed very far beyond the precincts of the camp. The town itself was off-limits. However, sentries weren't sufficient to keep the area under watch completely and some patrols would be sent out to check the various wine shops to find if anyone had slipped away from the camp unnoticed and gone drinking. Off we went anyway, the pair of us with our rifles on our shoulders and Paddy with his gun in his holster by his side. We came to the road where a Scotsman named Glavin[5] and another man were standing guard. Glavin raised a hand when he spotted us arriving and the other man stood to attention when he saw who was there. Glavin was swaying from side to side and began to stutter. Paddy stared carefully at the other man. 'Were you drinking too?' 'No, I wasn't,' he said holding himself as straight as a reed.

'Good.' Paddy turned his attention to Glavin.

'Hand me your rifle,' he ordered. Glavin indicated that he'd do everything according to the rules. He unloaded his rifle slowly and carefully as someone who was drunk might do, and once it was empty he proudly handed it over to Paddy. Paddy told me to go back to headquarters and tell Bill McGregor to send two men out to him immediately. The building that functioned as our headquarters was a few hundred yards away from us and I hurried back along in the darkness along a side-road that was full of holes and rocks. When I reached headquarters, I delivered the message to Bill McGregor straight away. Then I returned with both men. Glavin was arrested and locked up. He was just an innocent except when he got drunk and even then, all he did was act a bit stupidly. The smell of the wine was enough to make him drunk but he was never happy with just the smell of it.

We continued on then into the town. We went in and checked every wine shop and once we were happy that there was none of our group in any of them, we'd return home again. These wine shops were crowded with working men relaxing, drinking, smoking and chatting. We checked each place one after another, walked around it to have a look, and then moved onto the next one. You'd have to be one tough man to do all that checking without getting thirsty yourself. After a while I started giving Paddy the hint that the night was very warm and that I was parched and dying with the thirst etc. He didn't say anything. We arrived at the last bar; in we went, walked around, and checked out everyone who was in there. There was no one who wasn't there legally. We'd fulfilled our duties and responsibilities for the night. Paddy went straight up to the counter and myself and O'Regan followed him close behind. 'Tres vasos d'agua,' ('Three glasses of water') he says, the same as if he was issuing military orders! I couldn't refuse the water after saying that I was thirsty but to tell you the truth, I'd have preferred to stay thirsty than to drink water at that stage!

We were on parade one day. Paddy and Manuel were out in front of us. Paddy was explaining something to us and who arrived over to us suddenly but a young Spaniard who knew Manuel. Apparently, he'd just arrived at our camp and was delighted to see his friend again. As with those lorry drivers in Cervera, he didn't pay too much heed to the army of the Republic but ran straight over to Manuel and reached out to shake his friend's hand. Manuel just gave him a cold stare however and kept both his hands behind his back. He didn't say a word to him. A dejected look came over the young lad's face and he quickly lowered his hand, turned around and fell into the ranks again. That was Paddy and Manuel for you. Discipline and more discipline again!

Prior to Paddy joining our group, we'd been shown how to lay down our rifles on the ground suddenly and noisily. The phrase went: 'I want to hear the sound of the rifle striking the ground.' Paddy put a stop to this erroneous practice. He taught us how to leave the gun down gently. He taught us not to pull the trigger too suddenly but rather in a relaxed and smooth fashion holding your breath, in case the gun shook. He got very angry if he heard anyone saying 'pulling the trigger.' 'Squeezing it' – was what one should have said and done. To help people so that they didn't pull the rifle trigger too suddenly, and to make sure they pressed it or squeezed it in a more relaxed way, they used to place a small coin on the side of the empty rifle. Whenever the coin stayed in place after you pressed the trigger you knew you had it right. If the coin fell, you needed to practice more. One man who didn't manage this despite a lot of practice ended up being transferred to a machine-gun company so that his difficulties were sorted.

The food was bad at first in this place but after some complaints it improved. Party members were reluctant to complain and sometimes this reluctance was used against them. The small hotheaded man by the name of Frank Airlie was responsible for the improvement in the food. Neither his Party membership nor his loyalty prevented him from stirring things up if he thought it was needed. One day we were sitting together in a group outside on the ground, Paddy, Manuel and a Spanish Lieutenant (Teniente) were standing opposite us. The Lieutenant had only one hand – the consequence of some battle or other. The men began complaining about the food. Manuel, the interpreter, explained to the Spanish officer what they'd said. Frank Airlie jumped up and he was very annoyed. 'We didn't come here to eat pig's stuff!' Manuel translated this into Spanish; the officer got really angry. He stretched out his good hand and said something in a loud, defiant voice. When he'd stopped speaking Manuel said in English, 'He's asking who was it that referred to you as pigs?' There was silence for a moment. The teniente spoke again, giving us a fierce stare all the while. Again Manuel translated what he said into English, 'Show me the man that called you pigs.' Frank Airlie was sitting on the ground again. He didn't get up. He was a bit confused, I think. 'I never said,' he says in a low voice, 'that anyone called us pigs. I was referring to the food.' But he won out in the end, the same Frank. It was on account of what he said that the food improved from then on.

What remained of the company after the rout in Aragon was now based close to Tarragona where they were in the process of reorganising themselves. After we left Vilaseca we – the new recruits – made for the same camp as them. We spent a while in this camp undergoing various types of training; for the first time we had an opportunity to practice with hand grenades. Max Davies; a Welshman;[6] trained us in their use. 'I was a miner' he'd say, 'and I never thought that one day I'd be a soldier.' We were outdoors in the air and the battalion headquarters was in a building or compound close by. One night I was assigned to guard duty inside the gate of headquarters and given the password for entry into the compound. I locked the gate and took up my position on guard duty. Every now and then I'd hear footsteps passing outside on the road and fading into the distance.

> I gcoim na hoíche cloisim iad,
> Na coisithe ar siúl,
> (In the dead of night, I hear them,
> The walkers passing)

Those Irish-language words came back to me, that sliver of poetry that Tadhg Mac Firbisigh had taught us around ten years earlier in the technical school.

> Airím iad, ní fheicim iad,

46

Ní fios cá mbíonn a gcuairt.'
(I hear them, I cannot see them,
I know not where they call.)

Suddenly, someone knocked on the main gate and I went over to open the small door that was built into one side of it. It was a man from the battalion whom I didn't recognise.

'Listen,' he says, 'there's a man below in the camp who's very sick. I have to go in and see can I arrange to get help for him.'

'I can't let you in, I'm afraid,' I said. 'I have no authority to let anyone in without the password. That's the order I was given.'

'Don't you understand,' he says, 'this is an emergency? This comrade is in a bad way we don't know what's wrong with him but we need to get a doctor to him as soon as possible.'

I was unsure what to do.

'This may be a case of life or death', he says.

I let the man in and locked the gate behind him again. When he had everything sorted inside he came out again. I opened the small door for him and he went outside again. Then suddenly, just before leaving, he turns to me and says: 'That was very dangerous what you did there,' he says. 'Letting me in like that without a password. You should be more careful from now on!' Off he went as quickly again as he'd arrived. He left me standing there openmouthed staring after him in the darkness.

A small group of us were looking for permission to go out to a small village close by. Sam [Sam Wild, commander of the British Battalion] gave the pass to Bill Bibby. Bill looked at the piece of paper. 'You couldn't give us a later time than that for returning?' he says but Sam Wild's reply was a sharp one: 'You have to be back at the time stated there.' Without thinking, I blurted out a pun on his name to lighten the mood. 'It's not 'wild' enough for us, you see.' There was a momentary silence. The battalion leader gave me a frosty look, his thumbs in his belt where his gun was visible. He stared me up and down and then turned away. 'We've another clown here,' he probably said to himself.

On May Day, 1938, the government of Spain issued a statement known as *Los Trece Puntos* – (The Thirteen Points.) The historians of today say that the government sensed it didn't have the wherewithal to achieve a military victory and that by issuing this statement, they were indicating the least worst-case scenario they'd settle for in order to secure peace. Because of the military support Franco was getting from the dictators Hitler and Mussolini in respect of soldiers, technicians and war materials, he had all the advantages. This attempt at peace failed and the government had no choice but to continue with the war in the hope of some developments in the international situation. Soon after this, we heard that Daladier, the Prime Minister of France had closed down the border between France and Spain again, preventing the movement of war weapons and munitions to the Republic. He did this because of pressure from the British government. Our next training camp was in a place called Marçà, not far from Falset and closer still to the River Ebro. This is where we were really organised properly as a battalion and where we sensed the rigidity of military order and discipline more strongly than ever. We stayed in this camp longer than we stayed anywhere else and got most of our real training there. The British Battalion was now incorporated into the New Army of the Ebro and our mission, when we left this camp, was to cross the Rio Ebro and set Franco's army on the run. This Battalion comprised three infantry companies and one machine-gun company and about half of its members were Spaniards. The French government was busy imposing a range of new bans and proscriptions on us at this juncture, proscriptions that were tougher than ever so that new recruits could no longer get into Spain by crossing through the Pyrenees as before.

Consequently, to keep the Battalion going we had to recruit more Spaniards. We were living outside in the open countryside now and we had to build *chabolas* or little huts for ourselves for shelter; you had to clear the ground first and make it comfortable for lying down and then form a shelter made of branches and leaves and the likes. I gave a hand to a Cockney lad to put up *chabola* one evening and he was looking on carefully all the while.

'Have you ever worked on the roads before,' he asked?

'No, I didn't,' I replied but he continued staring at me doubtfully. He couldn't understand how I was so good at it. I didn't tell him that my father had been a gardener and that I'd often worked with him on different jobs – digging and shoveling. That clever Cockney had it right when he noticed that this wasn't the first time I'd handled a shovel. I didn't bother constructing a *chabola* for myself, however. Once night fell, I was happy enough to stretch my blanket out on the ground and lie down wherever I found a good spot. Bruce Boswell, the young Englishman who was involved in the Unity Theatre in London, styled this night ritual of mine – 'Kai Lung Unrolls His Mat.'[7]

One difficulty they had with the Battalion from the very beginning was what to call it? As regards to other nationalities, they were happy to accept any name really. The Americans – Abraham Lincoln; the Italians – Garibaldi; the Canadians – MacKenzie-Papineau; the Germans – Thälmann; the Yugoslav's – Dimitrov; the Poles – Dombrowski etc. No one managed to come up with a name that was acceptable to everyone in the British Battalion however. At one stage someone proposed the name Saklatvala – a communist who'd been in the Westminster Parliament during the 1920s. He was Indian by nationality – a 'red' Indian, so to speak! His name wasn't accepted as title for the battalion however. Every company had Irishmen in it. Paddy Sullivan was in charge of First Company. Bill McGregor was in the machine-gun company where Jack Nalty was in charge and Paddy Duff as his deputy. In Company No. 4 were Michael Lehane, James Haughey, James F. O'Regan, Hughie Hunter and myself. Other Irishmen scattered across the different battalions included Johnny Power, Waterford; Tom Murphy, Monaghan; Paddy Tighe, Mayo and many others. Paddy O'Daire from Donegal[8] was on the staff at headquarters but I only saw him rarely. Morris Davies was a Welshman and was in charge of Fourth Company; Bob Cooney, a Scotsman, was the battalion's political commissar. In truth, the 'Celtic Battalion' would have been a more accurate name for the column rather than the term 'British.'

My sergeant was an Englishman, Sergeant Proctor.[9] Proctor was a big cheerful, individual who was always in good form. Even when he was trying to act angry or fierce with you, he'd have a smile on his face.

Every morning after breakfast our rifles were examined to make sure the barrels were clean. (I'd a 1917 Remington initially.) I was a little bit lazy about this cleaning duty myself and I couldn't understand all the palaver about it. I just didn't see it as very important. The way I saw things, this was like cleaning a rusty knife in case the enemy got blood poisoning! We went through the same small show nearly every morning. I'd pull back the bolt and lift the rifle so Sergeant Proctor could examine the barrel and, next thing, it was: 'YOU NEVER CLEANED YOUR RIFLE, DOWNING!' Micheal Lehane was the direct opposite of me; he took very good care of his rifle and I often saw him caress it as one would do a lover. He was a real proper soldier.

Needless to say, it was really stupid of me not to clean the rifle properly. After you've used it for firing, tiny pieces of metal and dirt get stuck in the barrel and you need to clean these out or the rifle loses its accuracy.

Prior to this we did all our training out on the drilling square – the marching, firing and so on. Now we also began climbing every day. This was important preparation for the battles that lay ahead. We now focused on the use of arms and climbing and, crawling forward along the ground while under fire, twisting and turning. We were taught how to use light machine guns and tripods – how to take the tripod apart, how to set it up again and shooting, using the machine gun. Each infantry company had their own light machine gun – (a Diktarove or Degtyareva as it was known in Russian, I think). Our instructor in No. 4 Company for this gun was a Scotsman by the name of Anderson.[10] He was explaining something to us one day when an American interrupted him. The latter was a member of the British Battalion so I don't know why he wasn't in the Lincolns. This man was of Native American heritage or at least that's what he told us anyway. It'd be fair to say that he had hawk-like features and a certain noble bearing about him also. Anyway, an argument started between himself and Anderson. The American didn't agree with what the Scotsman was teaching us. Morris Davies, commander of No. 4 Company, heard the commotion and arrived over to us. 'What's wrong?', he says.

'This man's annoying me. I'm explaining to them how this gun works,' Anderson replies.

'He's not showing us how to do it properly,' the American says.

Davies gave him a fierce look. 'My advice to you,' he says, 'is to stop interrupting the instructor. Do you understand me?'

'He's still wrong', said the other man to himself in a low voice. Anderson continued with the lesson. After a while, he stopped and examined the gun carefully and said:

'Actually, now that I see it, this gun is a different type from what I originally thought. It's different in one way.' In the end, he had to admit that the Native American was right; the American was an expert in the use of that model of gun as it turns out.

The lack of food was the biggest issue affecting us, but I don't think this did us any harm in the long run. The opposite, maybe. I heard 'Happy' Cunningham saying that he'd never been as healthy in his life as he was there in Spain. We were given a hunk of bread every morning to last us for the day. I never did manage to cut this hunk of bread into three pieces – one for each part of the day. I'd all mine eaten first thing in the morning! Peas were our main food. We called them *beans* in English but chickpeas was the correct term for them.

We laughed when we heard that Bill Rust, the *Daily Worker's* correspondent in Spain reported that the British Battalion was 'full of beans!' Whenever we ate meat it was normally *burro* (or mule). One day it was my duty to divide out the food amongst the rest of the company and I received a good insight into the tendency that people have to lick up to those in authority. I was bent over the food that was in a big vessel on the ground and every plate that was passed in front of me I put a helping of food onto it. Someone put their plate in front of me and I ladled a dollop of food onto it. By chance, I happened to glance up at the same time and noticed that it was the company commander, Morris Davies. Before I could help myself I'd bent down again and given him an extra helping.

When I realised properly what I'd done and the pathetic reason for it I was annoyed with myself; it was too late by then.

Another bother for us was the lack of tobacco. Now and again Spanish cigarettes were divided out amongst us but the cigarettes were so strong and rough that we called them 'anti-tanks'! They reminded me of what they'd said back in Ireland about Father Sweetman when he'd had his tobacco-cultivation project at one time – 'Smoke Father Sweetman's tobacco and die for Ireland'. We used a cord dipped in saltpeter and a flint to light the tobacco. The men often used the same cords as belts to hold their trousers up. Usually, we were reliant on the cigarettes that people sent to us through the post but unfortunately they were often stolen before they reached us. All that was left by the time the letter arrived was the empty envelope and the smell of tobacco.

'If you get any cigarettes,' says an Englishman to O'Regan one day, 'think of me.'

'Yeah, sure, think of him', says Johnny Power, 'think of him but give them to me.' We tried to make cigarettes from vine leaves and I understood properly for the first time that old phrase in the Irish language that'd confused me when I'd heard it for the first time at school – 'ag ól tobac' (*lit:* to 'drink' (smoke) tobacco). This is proof I think that Irish-language speakers are descended from Spaniards orginally!

After a midday meal we were given some red wine to drink. This wine tasted bitter and very rough, so much so that after a few sips of it, you'd dump whatever was left over out on the rocks that stuck up out of the ground like a field in Connemara. The flies would be on the wine within seconds and having a good drink for themselves. A short while later and you'd see them swimming around drunkenly full of *vino rojo*. Much has been written over the years about the type of wine someone should drink with different meals. Anyway, this particular wine was so rough that it would have gone down well with a nice sod of turf!

Anyone who wasn't feeling well had to go to the medico's hut which was situated, naturally enough, at the top of the hill. We couldn't understand for the life of us why the medico didn't come down the hill to see to those who were sick however. If someone was only half-sick their 'prescription' was that they were set free from training that day and put on 'light work' instead – this to say pulling up hard pieces of scrub to use as firewood. Given that the ground was as hard as iron, you can see what I mean by the word 'light' in this context. Anyway, when I had a fever I had to be helped up to the top of the mountain and then 'brought to hospital' in a lorry. The 'hospital' was about mile away from the camp and it was really just a house that had been converted into a medical centre. I was put in a room that had two mattresses on the floor. There was a man lying on one mattress and I had the other. A German doctor was in charge and he had an American as his assistant. When I found out that the man lying next to me had gonorrhea it didn't do much to improve my fever, I can tell you! He was given an injection in the arse every day for his treatment. I wasn't given any medicine myself but the fever left me within a couple of days and I improved. I suppose it was the rest that cured me; additionally, although water was rationed we had washing facilities in this medical centre that we didn't have in the camp. Many of the infections we got probably came from the lack of washing facilities and the flies and insects and there was a strong link between flies and dysentery.

Once I was improved I left this house again without any formality and walked down the mountain again and back to the battalion. As I was walking down it struck me that I was a bit like Julius Caesar! In Shakespeare's play Cassius says referring to Caesar: 'In Spain,

Caesar had a fever, and it made him shake.' All I had to do to make it more real, I said to myself was travel to Italy and fall into the Tiber while I was at it!

There was an Englishman named Dunlop in the camp.[11] Prior to leaving England he was a teacher and he'd fluent Spanish. One day he was chatting with a group of Spaniards and all of a sudden he fell quiet. He was trying to think of a certain word but he couldn't bring the right Spanish term to mind – he had a blind spot, so to speak. I was just a few yards away, chatting with a few other lads. Dunlop turns around and says: 'What's the Spanish for "narrow"?' Strangely enough, I'd only memorised that word just the previous day in a sentence I found in Hugo's *Spanish Self Taught* – 'Esta demasiado estrecho' i.e. 'it is too narrow.' 'Estrecho', I replied.

'Oh, that's it,' he says. 'Thanks for that', and went back to his chat. The others were amazed at this. 'Who was this peasant from Ireland teaching people Spanish?' It was just a fluke, of course! But, chalk it down all the same – it was 'another point for Kerry' as my father used to say. Someone who has no knowledge at all of another language thinks that you're an expert, even if you've really only a few sentences of the language and you've learned them off by heart. It reminded me of a story I heard from my father when I was very young. He was captain of a GAA team in Blackrock just prior to the First World War, I think. A rule was set down that you couldn't be picked for the team unless you attended an Irish language class. There was one man there who was a brilliant player but had no interest in Irish. It goes without saying that he still played every Sunday despite this rule. But one Sunday another man who hadn't been picked for the team and who was very annoyed about it, gave him a dubious look. He says, 'You've no right to be on the team. You don't go to the Irish class.'

'Who doesn't go to the Irish class?'

'You don't – you can't speak Irish.'

'You can't.'

'Diggin too gewgawn?'

'Eh?'

'Diggin too gewgawn?'

'Oh, well, that's all right then – I didn't know you could speak Irish.'

I was standing guard at Battalion headquarters one night–it was my turn. Lewis Clive,[12] commander of No. 2 Company, passed by – a tall, straight-backed, serious-minded young man with an Oxford accent and a small walking cane under his arm as per usual. Shortly after this, I spotted Maurice Ryan and two others coming back down the road, returning to camp. They were in fairly good form and singing 'Nellie Dean'.[13] They walked past me shouting and acting the fool. I stayed where I was, angered at the side of the road, and watched them in a disinterested fashion. I didn't care one way or the other. After a short while I saw Maurice returning under armed guard however, he'd been arrested on Jack Nalty's orders and he was put in my charge until morning. He didn't cause any hassle but just lay down on the side of the path and promptly fell asleep. The following morning when I was ready to return to my company, he woke up and went in behind a bush to do his business. When he saw me leaving, he says, 'Will you bring me back my tin-plate from the camp? 'I'm finished with my shift here and I'm not coming back,' says I. Maurice could be very persuasive when he wanted to be, however. He pleaded with me for a while and so I gave in. 'Alright, where did you leave your tin?' I said, 'Is it near Jack Nalty's place?' Jack had found a cave on the side of a hill where he slept and I knew the place. 'That bollix?', he says angrily, 'no fear of it!' He couldn't stand John and the feeling was mutual. I suppose he felt that he should have been in charge of the machine-gun company and there was no doubt but that he was very able and certainly had the ability. He had a strong personality and he wasn't afraid of anyone. One day a row broke out between himself and Sam Wild and Wild says to him menacingly: 'You calling me a liar?'

'I'd call any man a liar,' says Ryan, without batting an eye, 'and I've the fear of my soul in me!' The pair of them faced off and Sam tried to stare Maurice down; he failed. Maurice had one weakness, however. He was fond of a drink and army discipline didn't suit him.

I was very friendly with an Englishman who was good at drawing cartoons, a man by the name of Bernard Burwell.[14] He told me one time that this wasn't his proper name and that he had no strong political views but that he was just in Spain for the adventure. He was an adventurer. It's difficult to understand why anyone would put their lives in danger if they didn't have strong philosophical or political beliefs. Burwell was a very direct and honest person. When a friend of his in England had heard that he was going to Spain and had decided to take part in the war there, he'd asked him why he was going. 'I told him,' he says to me, 'that I had the same motive as Prince Andrei in *War and Peace* when Pierre asked him that question. "I'm going to the war because the life I lead here is not to my taste."' One day I was about to praise one of his cartoons but something stopped me at the last minute and I changed my mind.

Ernest Gébler[15] had been in Connolly House, the headquarters of the Communist Party of Ireland, at some stage during the 1930s when he showed myself and Jim Prendergast a cartoon he'd drawn. He thought this cartoon of his would-be well-suited to the *Worker's Voice* but, as it happens, it wasn't accepted for publication. Anyway Prendergast looked at the picture that day and said: 'Isn't that amazing technique?'

'To tell you the truth,' says Gébler, 'the technique in it is terrible.' I'd been just about to praise the cartoon to the heights myself – only that Prendergast had interrupted me – and it's just as well that I didn't, I suppose. Consequently, when Bernard Burwell showed me this drawing of his, I said nothing, even if, privately, I thought it was really good. As the Bible says, I think, 'If a man saith nothing who shall accuse him afterwards that he hath said it?' Every few weeks, while our battalion was based there near Tarragona, some officer or other visited us notebook in hand and asking us questions. 'Anyone who hasn't a blanket, raise their hand…uno, dos, tres…okay. Anyone who hasn't a bayonet, raise their hand…uno, dos, tres…' And so on. Your man with the notebook would leave again and we wouldn't hear anything else about it. A few weeks later again and a different man appeared with his notebook. 'Anyone who hasn't a spoon, raise their hand. Uno, dos, tres…'

Paddy Tighe (Mayo)

As for this Red Indian here's another short anecdote I remember about him. We were walking in a single line one day along a narrow path up the side of a mountain when we came to a small little field. The sun was shining on something in the middle of the field and the Red Indian thought it might be a medal or a coin of some description. He went into the field for a look and came out again a minute or two later. Whatever it was – it turned out to be something worthless; it was just whatever way the sun was shining on it. Out of the blue, a local farmer appeared and began to berate him in Catalan. He thought that this man was trying to steal some of his onions apparently. Our comrade didn't bother saying anything in response and we went on our way. Seeing as we – the *Internacionales* – were in Spain trying to protect people like this farmer and fighting on their behalf, it bothered me to think that the man might think any of us were trying to rob him. 'Why didn't you explain to your man that you weren't trying to steal his food?', I said. But he just shrugged as much as to say that he couldn't care less what the farmer thought.

One night when I was about to go sleep, the crack of a rifle sounded nearby. A few minutes later and Michael Economides our company commissar arrived in; he bent down and asked me in a whisper did I know who was responsible for the shot. 'I was half-asleep when the shot went off' I said, 'but I think it came from the other side of the camp near the machine-gun company.' 'I saw the flash over here though' he said, leaving again. The following morning I heard that the Red Indian's rifle had accidentally gone off and his gun was just a few yards away from where I was sleeping at the time!

We were given new rifles. Initially, the rumours going around were that they'd come from Russia; and then the word was that they'd come from Czechoslovakia. Who knows? I preferred the old rifles we'd had previously as the bolts could be pulled over and back more easily on them. These new ones [Soviet Nagant] were very stiff. We sang rebel songs sometimes when we were out marching to overcome boredom. The one that I liked best went like this:

> Hitler and Franco your future is black
> Workers' battalions are driving you back
> Sons of the masses forever will be
> Forward red soldiers to victory

As O'Regan said to me cynically once, 'Every time Franco takes over another town, we sing "Hitler and Franco your future is black!"' That put me in mind of the time when I'd been in Croke Park at a match one day. Kerry were way ahead of Dublin in this match and a low-sized Dublin man was standing beside me. And every time Kerry got a point he'd shout out: 'Come on Dublin. Yez have them groggy!' And that man had the right idea, of course. He was doing his best to perk up the team he supported and to encourage their players. In much the same way, whenever we sang 'Hitler and Franco, your future is black', we'd finish with a shout and a challenge 'Up the Republic!'

Domingo Morales was always singing one particular song and when I heard it again at a later stage, I recognised it as the same tune that he had. This was actually a ballad that had originated in Aragon but a new version of it had been written in honour of the 15th International Brigade.

We weren't always singing rebel songs, needless to say. Sometimes, protest songs were sung highlighting some injustice or other – the type of song that you'd expect from the soldiers in any army trying to let off steam. While waiting patiently in line for food one day, some of the group began singing:

> Waiting waiting, waiting,
> Always bloody well waiting,
> Waiting in the morning, waiting in the night
> Waiting, waiting, waiting,
> Always bloody well waiting,
> God send the day what we'll bloody well wait no more.

Paddy O'Sullivan didn't like that song at all: 'Can you not think of something else to sing besides that?', he'd ask unhappily. Most political commissars have a bad reputation. They are normally depicted as merciless men who are always threatening prison and death on others or searching for political heretics or those who might betray the cause. But that wasn't how it was at all. The main duty that the commissars had was to educate us on political issues and current affairs and to initiate debates and discussions on same. Given that this war in Spain was closely intertwined with international affairs at the time, we always had a great deal of interest in European matters and developments. In October, 1936 the Spanish government issued a proclamation stating that it was the political commissars' duty to explain the objectives of the war and the government policies relating to it – without simultaneously interfering with or undermining their military leadership. The commissar also functioned as an intermediary between each soldier and their battalion's leadership. He could sort out minor problems or penalize people for minor misdemeanors or infractions without having to impose the full rigors of military discipline.

There was a Greek from Cyprus in our company and one day an argument developed between himself and an Englishman. The Englishman berated him and called him a 'greasy Greek'. This man went to Michael Economides,[16] the Company Commissar (he was a

Cypriot himself as it happens) to make a complaint. Economides took the Englishman aside and discussed the issue with him in a nice calm way: 'The man never thought he'd hear an insult the likes of this in the International Brigade. He was expecting a higher standard than that.' The Englishman was embarrassed and ashamed about what he'd said and apologised.

Another man had a problem with his shoes that were pinching him and hurting him and so he took them off one day and threw them into the ditch instead of bringing them back to camp with him. Economides spoke to him in the same quiet way and the issue was sorted out. Many minor issues and arguments were sorted out like this so that people were embarrassed in a political way rather than having the full might of military discipline enforced on them.

I complained myself at one stage – the only complaint I ever made. We had a barber there who was a Spaniard and because he had to be at work, shaving and cutting hair when the rest of us were finished our work for the day – he was off between morning and evening. But for three nights in a row, while I was waiting for a haircut, he closed the shop. He was happy enough to abandon his station once he had all his friends shorn and shaved. 'Es terminado, camarada.' 'Right so,' I said to myself, 'I'll *terminado* you, mister.' I went straight in to Michael Economides and explained the situation to him. He listened to me carefully without saying a word. But what I said produced results. The following morning, your man was outside in the ranks again, a sheepish look on his face – drilling and climbing the same as all the rest of us. So, there were times when the commissar didn't have the power to protect whoever was accused of something and wasn't able to smooth things over.

Every morning after the inspection of the different companies the entire battalion came together and the various orders for that day were read out – the work scheme etc. This was read out in Spanish whenever a Spaniard was the officer in charge and in English whenever it was an English-speaker. One day, Domingo Morales, a young Spanish officer, was issuing the orders when, suddenly, he was interrupted by a loud shout from First Company, someone with a strong Scottish accent saying 'SAY IT IN ENGLISH!' A second later a clear and authoritative voice called out: 'ARREST THAT MAN!' The Scotsman had a hangover after going out drinking the night before and he hadn't recovered yet. In this situation, the commissar couldn't do anything to help the Scotsman. And the second man who'd called out? It was none other Paddy O'Sullivan! I'd say Paddy was the best officer in the Battalion during my time there from the point of view of keeping order and discipline and also in terms of his military knowledge and his overall personality. He never lost his cool, nothing ever stressed him and he always knew what to do no matter how unexpected the situation. Referring to him sometimes when he was out of earshot, various members of the company had a habit of saying 'that bollix!' This was just bravado and pretence, however. They had huge respect for O'Sullivan and if asked 'What company are you in?' they'd respond proudly – 'I'm in O'Sullivan's company', as much as to say that this was a special company. People who weren't suited to discipline and order would say against him that he was like a sergeant in a 'bourgeois army.' Sometimes you'd hear a shout from him, the likes of this: 'THAT'S NOT A SORE DICK YOU HAVE IN YOUR HAND, IT'S A RIFLE!' But O'Sullivan got results that were evident for all to see. To be honest, he'd have made a good soldier out of a corpse!

I'll never forget one day that Paddy left the entire battalion waiting for him outside. The Battalion was ordered to fall in on the parade ground for an announcement from Battalion Commissar, Bob Cooney.[17] When the appointed time arrived however, every company was present and in their ranks except First Company. Everyone was curious about the reason for the meeting. Above us – on a piece of raised ground – stood Sam Wild, Commander of the Battalion and Bob Cooney. Slightly to one side of them stood a battalion member who'd been arrested for something and two armed men on either side of him, guarding him. It was obvious from the shocked look on the prisoner's face that he couldn't believe he'd been arrested – what am I doing here? What have they arrested me for etc.?

A short distance away, somewhere in the background, Paddy's voice could be heard calling out orders and issuing instructions. A few minutes passed and the only thing that broke the silence was the sound of Paddy's voice giving his group orders. Sam Wild was not a patient man – the exact opposite in fact. He looked at his watch, then called over one of his runners and ordered him to tell Paddy O'Sullivan to get over to the parade ground with his company double-quick! The man left with the message and returned almost as soon again. Another few minutes passed and by now, Sam Wild was fit to be tied. But just as he was about to explode, Sullivan appeared on the parade ground at the head of *la primera compañia*. The men took their place in the ranks and Paddy glanced up at the battalion leader and the commissar nice and relaxed – as much as to say 'You can go ahead now with whatever business you have in hand!' We found out afterwards that Paddy was unhappy with something they were doing as part of his company's drills and that he wouldn't join the others until his company had followed every instruction of his fully and to the letter.

But to go back to the military court and the man they'd imprisoned that day. What happened was that he'd written a letter home and it hadn't gone down well with whoever had read it. The Battalion had its own system of censorship in place and this man had complained about this and that – the usual minor complaints that every army member has – anywhere in the world. So the commissar read the letter out in front of the entire Battalion and gave a running commentary all the while. 'You know all about it,' the man had written to his friend back in England, 'you know the sacrifices I made to come over here.' The commissar fell quiet after he'd read out this sentence and scanned the crowd gathered on the parade ground. 'When I read that,' he says, 'I checked out this fellow's background. I thought he might have been a bank manager or something back home but instead, I discovered that he was a general labourer.' On this occasion, it seemed to me that the commissar went over the top by publicly shaming the prisoner like that – and the very minor reason for the man's complaint. Publicly criticizing someone in this way and democracy just didn't tally right in my view. Anyway, the poor man was assigned to a work squad; I'd say that was the least of his punishments that day.

The only mistake the commissars made, it seems to me, was that they decided to organise a small group of people to secretly act as 'activists' for them. Certain people were chosen for this small group whose duty it was to secretly make sure that no one was going off-kilter in terms of their political views or was scheming or dissenting against the Battalion's leadership in the background. It's impossible to keep something like that secret however and once the word got out, the men were very angry. Everyone knew exactly what the idea behind this was – despite the political 'explanations' that the leadership later gave them – it was obvious to all that this was just a system of spying set up behind people's backs and that the 'activists' had to report back every form of dissent or unhappiness to headquarters. And it wasn't just the people who'd been 'kept out of the scheme of things' that were strongly opposed to this form of spying and felt uneasy about it, but also many of the 'true believers' themselves. The whole thing was stupid and damaging and the men opposed it to such an extent that the leadership soon gave up on the whole idea. While the 'activists' idea received a lot of criticism, it's important to say that it wasn't out of badness that the leadership came up with this plan in the first place but from over-enthusiasm instead. Any unhappiness or apparent dissent amongst the men related to minor issues – the same as in any army. And it's a healthy thing really to be able to get your complaints and grievances off your chest and let off a bit of steam. In reality, the only thing that would have come of this plan was a lowering of morale amongst the men and this would have been the exact opposite of what they'd sought to achieve in the first place.

It was generally accepted that the best time to get rid of lice was during official announcements or political speeches. As the funny-men in the battalion used to say – this way we wouldn't be wasting any time! When Jack Nalty gave a lecture to No. 4 Company on the Irish Volunteers during the War of Independence, their objectives, their training and their system of organisation and discipline everyone listened carefully to it. Jack spoke in a direct and simple style without any trace of political posturing and his talk got high praise from everyone. While the lecture was going on, I noticed Paddy O'Sullivan trotting up and down outside on the road on the back of a horse.

Wolfe Tone Commemoration

In June the Irish members of the battalion organised a Wolfe Tone Commemoration. We were given permission to organise a *fiesta* of our own in the evening and everyone contributed a certain amount of pesetas to the kitty so as to buy food and drink. It was easy enough to get our hands on wine back then but as for food…? This was a problem. But we found a solution to this. An American battalion, known as the Lincolns, was located in the same area as us and the Yanks have a name for being able to get their hands on anything you need. Compared to us, they always seem to have their choice of food and drink and they didn't smoke the 'anti-tanks' and had Chesterfields and Lucky Strikes instead. They had their own canteen and Bill McGregor bought a quarter-side of tinned bacon and bread from them. We made sandwiches for the party also. The big night came around and we all gathered together. Bill asked Paddy O'Sullivan to be in charge of the fiesta and he was happy to do this. As Bill said in a letter he wrote home to his mother at the time, 'We felt that since vino would be in attendance a strong military man was essential for this job.'

Strange to say, there were far more Irishmen in the battalion that night than we thought there were! Even some of the Spaniards became Irish for the night. From the foreigners among us, we heard songs such as 'It's the Rich wot gets the Pleasure, the Poor wot gets the Blime' and 'Buddy, can you Spare a Dime?' You'd have thought that songs like this mightn't have been particularly suited to the occasion but in a way, they really suited the event – because, wasn't Wolfe Tone sympathetic to 'the people who were poor'? Michael Lehane had a habit of explaining the background and history as relating to every Irish ballad and every poetic image they contained. The historical explanation to the song was more important than the song itself, the way he saw it. Once the *fiesta* finished that night,

I don't think there was anyone there who didn't know all about Róisín Dubh, Caitlín Ní Uallacháin and the Seanbhean Bhocht. Anyone who was still ignorant about them by then – it was their own fault! The craic had an international flavour to it as well. A young Scotsman did a Cossack dance and it's easier to say the word 'Cossack' than to dance the dance after you've been drinking, believe me! Halfway through the fun and games we discover that the sandwiches – or what were left of them – had disappeared. In the slang used back then – 'they'd been "looked after".' By now however, food wasn't something that was bothering us anymore and we continued with our drinking and singing songs. I suppose that there was a certain element of nationalist sentimentality as regards the songs we sang, but I suppose this is a habit of the Irish. Anyway, suffice to say, that songs and ballads from every corner of Ireland rang out and across the Catalan hills that night as we paid our respects to Wolfe Tone. When the party was over and we were ready to hit the hay, I spotted Sam Wild a short distance from us in the half-darkness looking on quietly – just in case. He needn't have worried however. The general consensus – as Bill said in the letter I mentioned earlier – was that it was 'the best conducted fiesta yet held.'

Pandit Nehru

Sometimes, well-known people paid us a visit. Pandit Nehru [Indian nationalist leader, India's first Prime Minister] paid us a visit at one stage.[18] He didn't give any speech but walked around the camp and chatted informally with everyone. A machine-gun demonstration was organised in his honour for the occasion. A few hundred yards away, on the hillside that was on the other side of the glen, stood a group of trees. Maurice Ryan from Limerick was able to knock slivers off these trees with a Maxim machine gun – even from a good distance away. He was the best marksman amongst us. O'Regan got Nehru to sign his name in a copy of a book that Frank Ryan edited in Madrid – *The Book of the XV International Brigade*. When Nehru realised that we were Irish, as he chatted with us, he told us that he'd visited Dublin in 1907, I think. He also said that the nationalist movement in Ireland had been a huge inspiration for Indian nationalists.

At one stage during our chat with Nehru, Michael Lehane made reference to the Fenians and David Guest's[19] ears pricked up on hearing this. Guest was an intellectual. He had read a good deal and was very knowledgeable on many different subjects. 'Did you know,' he says 'that Charles Dickens had a dog that he called "The Fenian"?' We hadn't heard this. 'Someone gave this bloodhound to him as a present and the dog hated the colour red. And whenever the Redcoats were marching past on their way from Gravesend to Chatham, the dog would run out and attack them so viciously that they'd have to run for cover. Therefore, Dickens named his dog "The Fenian." They had to put the dog down in the end.'

'What did I tell you,' says Michael Lehane joking. 'Death without a priest!'

Whatever chat we had after that, David made a sarcastic reference to the English writer Middleton Murry at one stage.

'Katherine Mansfield married him all the same,' piped up one man.

'That means nothing,' says David, 'many a good woman has thrown herself away on a rotter.'

The book I referred to was issued by *The Commissariat of War* in Madrid and it was announced that a copy of it was going to Moscow as a present for Stalin from the [15th] Brigade – and Brigade members could sign their names in it if they wished to do so. When the book came round to me, I wrote my name in Irish. In my mind's eye, I saw Stalin looking through the list of names carefully as he sat there comfortably in the Kremlin smoking his pipe. 'Who's this fellow, Eoghan Ó Duinnín [Eugene Downing]?', I heard him asking. 'This man understands the national question and he should be awarded the Order of Lenin!'

A rumour went around that Franco was dead.

'Well,' says Michael Lehane, 'if it's true, then there's no harm reciting the poem Byron composed on hearing Castlereagh had died:

> Posterity will ne'er survey
> A nobler grave than this.
> Here lie the bones of Castlereagh,
> Stop traveller – and piss!
> *Death without a priest?*

Shortly before we crossed the Ebro, a certain Irishman asked – 'Will there be a priest available at the front?' The dogs in the street knew that the clergy were looking after the opposition, the pagan Moors included. Therefore, everyone thought this was a joke. But the man's question didn't surprise me one bit. I understood the situation of the Irishman who is against the church and views it as an organization that hinders the people's development and is always on the side of the rich – this despite all the encyclicals – but (i.e. the man) isn't an atheist at the same time. This is the conflict that anti-clerical Republicans always have and so they create a religion of their own that allows them to serve both sides. They are Catholics as they see it but they don't pay any attention to the bishops. There's no rhyme or reason to this philosophical perspective as I see it. If it is true that the church was divinely instigated and provides divine guidance in this world, then she cannot be wrong about anything, can she? Because that's like saying that God has gone astray or is in error. And indeed, there were many times through history that the church made errors given that she is a human endeavor – and as with any organisation or association she can get things right or wrong. One has no choice other than to be a believer or an atheist. One has to choose one or the other. But then again, maybe there is a third way when all is said and done. 'Are you a Christian?', as the priest said to the man. 'No,' he says, 'but I am a Connacht man.'

Eugene Downing with other members of the British Battalion of XV International Brigade just before the Ebro crossing

Photograph of members of British battalion just before crossing the Ebro. Eugene Downing is on the left wearing glasses

P55/7

 República Española

Número de la libreta *98374*

Brigadas Internacionales

CARNET MILITAR PARA

Apellidos *DOWNING*

Nombre *Eugene*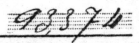

LEER CON ATENCION

1) Se ruega a los camaradas que a cada cambio, su Unidad haga la inscripción correspondiente.
2) No se extienden duplicados de este Carnet.
3) Los portadores del Carnet no tienen derecho a hacer inscripciones.

— 1 —

First page of Eugene Downing's military ID

P55/9

INSPECCIÓN GENERAL DE SANIDAD MILITAR
SERVICIO DE ESTADÍSTICA

ES
Mod 5

FICHA MÉDICA DE HOSPITALIZACIÓN

Núm.

FILIACIÓN

Apellidos *Downing*
(Se consignarán los dos)
Nombres *Eugen*
(El primero y las iniciales de los demás)
Unidad a que pertenece *15. brig*   Grado

Datos del reclutamiento   Núm. de la chapa

Residencia de la familia *Irlandia*

Sellos de los Hospitales con la fecha de entrada y salida

1.ª Entrada	2.ª Entrada	3.ª Entrada	4.ª Entrada
	Salida por	Salida por	Salida por

DIAGNOSTICO	Inicial	Terminal
H.a.f. piernas izq.		*Amput. pierna izq. ulcers en brazo der.*
Región anatómica afecta	*Piernas izq. – Brazo der.*	
Tejidos ú órganos lesionados		
Agente vulnerante	*bala.*	
Terminación por	el día de	de

Imprenta de A. Ortega.-Barcelona

Document on amputation

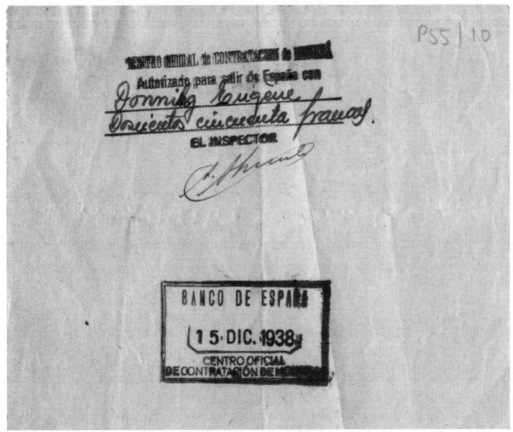

Issue of 250 French Francs on leaving Spain

CHAPTER 5

TO THE EBRO

Two women, a mother and a daughter, were passing outside on the road one day, carrying a bundle of clothes on their back.

'Tienes jabón?', the mother calls out.

'Tienes huevos?', someone from the battalion says in reply.

'No tenemos,' says the woman.

'No jabón', says the man.

(Have you any soap? Have you got eggs? No; No, we have no soap.)

Michael [Lehane] overheard this exchange and he looked around where various things are scattered on the ground here and there – as we were getting ready to leave camp. He found a bar of soap and hurried back up the road to catch up with them and give them the soap. He didn't know that anyone else had noticed him doing this.

We left Marçà and moved closer still to the Ebro. *El nuevo Ejército del Ebro* (The New Army of the Ebro) was gathering there and preparing to engage the enemy in battle on the other side of the river. We spent our last night prior to the attack – Sunday night, 24 July 1938, camped on a very rough and rocky stretch of ground. The ground was rough but we slept soundly that night all the same. 'Weariness can snore upon the flint'.[1]

In April, 1938 Franco had reached the Mediterranean and the Spanish Republic was torn in two – with Franco's forces threatening Valencia and Sagunto, the Republic was now in grave danger. But when the Republican army crossed the Ebro – in a line that stretched from Mequinenza to Amposta – a distance of about 60 miles, Franco had no option but to bolster his forces with extra men. His momentum stalled and he couldn't effect his planned attack against Valencia. After two days of fierce fighting, about 400 miles squared was under Republican control and we'd taken 5,000 prisoners. Our offensive succeeded in the initial phase. But because of his extra weapons and supplies, Franco put a stop to our progress just before Gandesa and that's when the real slaughter began. With the help of his bomber planes and his big guns, every hill and stretch of land was razed with constant bombing and shelling. Franco had plenty of metal at his disposal he pounded the whole region with it. Following fierce and bloody fighting that continued incessantly for more than four months, Franco retook the land that the Republic had gained within a few days. As Manuel Tagüena wrote in his *Memorias*, the Battle of the Ebro, it was

> una mission de sacrificio…Debiamos parar la ofensiva del enemigo sobre Valencia y ganar tiempo hasta que la situación en Europa evolucionara a nuestra favor.
> (A sacrificial mission…We had to hinder the enemy's attack on Valencia and buy time until the European political situation turned in our favour.)

This in a very few short words is the story of the Battle of the Ebro. Eventually the big day came – that defining day that was Monday 25 July 1938 when – according to the military experts – the biggest and bloodiest battle of the Spanish Civil War took place. 50,000 men took part in this attack of ours. As it turned out, it was also 'el dia de la Fiesta de Santiago Apostól, el Patrona de España' that day.[2] Not that this was the reason that we arranged our attack for that day; instead, it was because the night was as black as pitch – so dark that there was no sign of light at all in the sky.

After we'd eaten our meal we were ready to head out onto the main thoroughfare and march on towards the banks of the river. Just as we set off, we heard that the attack had already begun and that the Republican Army forces were already on the other side of the Ebro. The Moroccans were on the retreat. We'd caught them by surprise. Shells hurtled over our heads and exploded somewhere behind us but no one was hurt. We gathered together on the road and stood there for a while as the machine gunners overtook us, their big guns under their arms. They whistled happily as they passed us on the road. Then, once the road was clear, we moved on.

On our way into battle that day, I was carrying a rifle, some loose bullets and two hand grenades in addition to a roll of bandage. Just as we reached the banks of the river, an enemy plane zoomed in over us, spraying us with machine-gun fire and we threw ourselves flat on the ground.

'Nil illegitimo carborundum,' shouts Yorkie.[3]

'What's that?', I said, crouching down behind a bush. 'Don't let the bastard grind you down,' he says. Once the danger had passed, we went on again until we reached the river where Catalan fishing boats were moving over and back, ferrying men across the Ebro. Each boat held eight men, with the local fishermen themselves rowing the boats. Soon we were on the other side – even if we'd yet to fire a shot. We crawled up the riverbank and regrouped again out on the road. A fine wide road stretched out in front of us as blanketed by fields on both sides – and there wasn't sight or sound of anyone. We passed a water pump on the side of the road and stopped to refill our water bottles. It was a moment of high emotion and great hope, a special moment. Bob Cooney, our surly Scotsman (normally) battalion commissar, stood right there in the middle of the road, his arms folded, his face lit up in a great smile as we all filed past. He was really enjoying the entire adventure – and it was going so well. We left the middle of the road clear and moved on, flanking both sides of the road in two lines. Now and again, the roar of the bomber planes came our way again and we scattered, disappearing into the ditches and flattening ourselves against the earth until the danger had passed. Funnily enough, we actually welcomed the appearance of the odd plane overhead because it gave us a chance to have rest and get some shade from the boiling sun. It wasn't very dangerous either when the bombers passed over because we lay down flat in the ditch immediately and all their pilots saw were empty roads in front of them.

A group of prisoners passed us under armed guard. They showed no loyalty to Franco – the opposite, in fact. 'Salud, camaradas!', they called out as they passed us. They didn't look devastated or horrified to be captured at all. They were Spaniards or Italians, I can't remember exactly now. Anyway, there was no doubt but that they were delighted to be finished with the fighting. Our group officer, George Fletcher [battalion adjutant], appeared on horseback and declared excitedly: 'We have the bastards on the run!' The shortest communiqué ever communicated in a war situation!

It was incredibly hot at this stage, the sun beating down and splitting the rocks. We began to suffer from thirst again. I was so hot that I threw away my blanket. I just couldn't carry it any more even if I was probably breaking some military regulation or other, by throwing it away like this. Now and again we came across a dead mule lying on the side of the road, and we'd make a joke about it – 'There's tomorrow's dinner!' Suddenly, a burst of gunfire sounded and there were bullets exploding and whistling all around – as we discovered that the odd hill here and there was still under enemy control, even if the majority of the enemy had made a run for it. We had to retake these hills before going on further. At one stage, Michael Economides told us that there was no point in ducking down suddenly once you heard the crack of gunfire as – in that second – the bullets had already passed you. Funnily enough, just a minute or two after he told us this, we were sprayed with gunfire from somewhere on an incline nearby. Before he could help himself, Michael instinctively ducked down, alongside everyone else! In fairness, to him, Economides joined in the laughter at this – the same as all the rest of us. We left the road and re-captured one of the hills with little difficulty. A while later and an order reached us, 'Get ready. We're going to attack the hill directly opposite us.' We waited for the go-ahead but it never came. Time passed. Whatever led to the delay, we weren't sure but the sun begin to set as night drew in. Another few hours passed and it was too dark to mount an attack. The light disappears quickly in Spain especially – and so too does the heat – especially when you're on higher ground. I was sorry now that I didn't have my blanket. I was on first watch for No. 4 Company that night and even if the sky was pitch-black and I couldn't see a thing, I stared down into the glen and listened carefully for any sign of the enemy – in case they tried to launch an attack on us under the cover of darkness. It's a big responsibility to have when a group of men are relying on you to protect them against a surprise ambush. It's not easy to keep your imagination under control, and it's incredible how anxious you get on hearing every strange and unfamiliar sound the night makes.

The following morning, we found out that the Americans had already taken this hill the day before and that it'd been under our side's control throughout the night. We were lucky that we hadn't made a terrible mistake and launched an attacked the previous evening – such mistakes often occur in war.

On we went again next day towards Corbera and Gandesa where the Fifteenth Corps intended assembling – as planned by the leadership. Before long, we were to engage another small group of the enemy – they were Moors – there were still small bands of them here and there, probably in an effort to delay our advance. In one of these skirmishes, Frank Airlie lost an arm. He was badly injured in a hail of machine-gun fire and the medical people had no option but to amputate the arm from the shoulder – immediately. It was on a stretcher that poor Frank began his return journey back across the Ebro and onto the hospital in Mataró. Now that we'd various small groups of enemy 'cleaned up' we could advance more quickly. We were now marching in the direction of Gandesa where it was obvious from the noise that the real battle was in full swing; the skirmishes were over now. A light armoured car came towards us from the front-line and gave us the latest information on what was happening. We'd taken Corbera, a small town situated at the bottom of La Sierra de Caballs, about five miles from Gandesa. The enemy still had a firm grip on the hills fronting this important Catalan centre however and without getting control of these hills, there was no way that we could get control of this important town. Further on we left the road and began climbing in the hills again. It was tough going, climbing against the slope and you couldn't but be put in mind of that phrase of Peadar O'Donnell's during the 1930s: 'the high ground of the Republic'. And there was no shortage of 'high ground' in this area either. We were now in a region where you found: 'las zonas más elevades de la región'. We climbed higher, one after another as the bullets and shells came thick and fast. Luckily for us, the shells were coming from too far away to do us any serious damage. Those shelling us didn't have the right range yet. Closer we came to reaching the peak of the hill and we began to pass dead bodies here and there. The first corpse I saw was lying face-down, his two hands stretched out on the ground like someone having a rest. The man wasn't dead long as I overheard two men close by, one of them saying: 'I did warn him about his water-bottle and the way he left it uncovered like that.' Apparently, the sun had been shining on the metal of the bottle. An enemy sniper had used this as his target and the bullet had gone straight through the bottle and killed the man instantly. A Moor probably – they were very good snipers.

We moved on, following on one another's heels. Suddenly the column came to stop where there was a gap in the hill – about five yards in width – the men were reluctant to go forward as they'd be momentarily exposed and completely unprotected from enemy fire. Morris [Davies] hurried up to us.

'What's the delay?' he says. 'What's wrong?'

The men explained the situation to him.

'On you go,' he says gruffly. 'There's no danger here. Come on!'

Next thing, Morris walks ahead and stands right in the middle of the gap! Completely unafraid, he stood there, his arms held out in the shape of a cross, the sound of firing loud all the while – the whistle of bullets and the explosion of shells all around us. He just stood there momentarily like that without saying a word – almost as if he was trying to be killed! 'They can't see this place,' he says – urging the men forward again. Maybe he knew that we were safe from enemy fire there – i.e. that this was not a 'maw of danger'[4] but it was still a brave man who would do what he did then! We reached a small plateau or bank of ground just beneath the peak of the hill but to fire on the enemy ensconced on the hill opposite us –which was the last point of defence for Gandesa, we had to go up higher again, right up to the very top. One man looked up and he didn't like what he saw.

'There's no cover from enemy fire up there at all,' he says.

'That's madness, those bushes won't stop any bullets. We'll be slaughtered!' Sergeant Proctor arrived and said: 'Up you go and start firing at them or I'll put this bullet right into your head' – that quiet smile on his face all the while. We advanced again and stretched flat on the ground, we got our range and began firing at the enemy line on the other side of the glen. On one side of me was James O'Regan and the other was the Cockney.

It was only the previous morning that we'd crossed the river and captured 5,000 prisoners and moved more than 20 miles into opposition territory but now, the enemy was beginning to recover and regroup and our attempt to 'catch them by surprise' had no effect at this stage. Franco was given the bad news that *el enemigo ha pasado el Ebro* and he began to fortify his defensive line; he had the arms and munitions at his disposal to do that.

CHAPTER 6

AS A HOSPITAL PATIENT

We were firing on the enemy continuously now as instructed. Our fire was being returned and, all of a sudden, I felt a burning feeling as a bullet went straight through my left leg! James O'Regan helped me down as far as the small bank of ground just below the peak of the hill so that the medical people could see to me. The pain was fairly bad in the beginning but after a while it eased a bit. They put a tourniquet on my leg but warned me not to 'leave it on any longer than a quarter-of-an-hour without changing it for fear of gangrene.'

The sounds of battle outside continued all the while but it grew quieter indoors as some of the most badly-wounded men died. Just that low agonized moaning of those who needed medical treatment and the medical attendants talking amongst themselves. Most of the medical people were Americans and, at one stage I heard one of them say that Franco's soldiers had left a lot of tinned food behind them. A can of sweet milk was opened and handed to me. We heard the noisy clatter of heavy machinery passing by out on the road. 'That's the big guns going up to the front,' the Americans told us. That was how my first night there went by – listening to all the different sounds and human voices indoors and the impersonal racket of battle in the distance outside. An American voice again: 'That dog that was sniffing around. I'd to put him down in case he got the taste of human flesh.' I was put on a stretcher and began my journey back down the mountain again, two Spaniards carrying the stretcher. The path down was so steep and sharp however that I had to keep a tight hold of the stretcher in case I tumbled out on the ground. Whenever the shells came too close, the two men had to drop the stretcher suddenly and lay themselves flat on the ground – not that I could blame them! Eventually we reached our destination; it was huge relief to me and to us that we'd made it back down again in one piece. I was back in Corbera again, the small town I mentioned earlier, where a building had been specifically laid aside for those who'd been wounded in the fighting. Injured men lay all on the floor all over the place and every few minutes more and more men were carried in and the place was soon full of wounded soldiers. It was starting to get dark now. The light was very weak; it was just a few oil lamps I think. And you could hear the low incessant moaning of the severely wounded coming from all corners of the building. A young lad close beside me was calling out pitifully, over and over again – 'Madre mia, mi madre!' Not long afterwards, this lad went quiet and a medical attendant looked down at him and checked him, then pulled the blanket up over his face. There were other men there who died very soon after their arrival, they were so badly injured. It was heartbreaking. All you could hear were their voices crying out in agony – 'Medico! Medico!', and always the same reply – 'No medico aquí'.

Shortly before daybreak, all the men who were still alive were placed in ambulances and we went back in the direction of the river. From my stretcher, I could see that the vines were beginning to ripen on either side of the road – green and black – as were the figs and the nectarines. All the fruit-gatherers had left, it goes without saying.

We were making for the Hospital de Sangre in Mataró. This had been a college before – el Colegio Valldemia under the direction of Los Hermanos Maristas. We congregated together at the river, everyone who'd been wounded but could still walk, and the stretcher cases. I only spotted the odd person from my own company in this group. The Scotsman Anderson was there; he'd been injured in the hand. We crossed the river on a big raft that was operated by a large cable stretched from one side of the river to the other, with another wire going from the raft up to this bigger cable, so that the current couldn't pull the raft off-course. The wire from the raft was fixed to the larger cable with a giant slip-knot and operated by a type of pulley-system.

A major problem occurred once we'd all been loaded onto the raft. Whatever happened, the main cable got jammed and we couldn't move. The men in charge began to hit the cable with big sticks to try and loosen it but they couldn't get it to shift; it was stuck fast. The rest of us looked up anxiously from where we lay on our stretchers because 'there was death in the sky' now that it was fully daylight. It wouldn't be long before Franco's planes arrived and began their shooting and bombing, and we'd be rightly caught – like rabbits in the headlights. Next minute, a Spanish lieutenant appeared on the scene, a man who'd only one arm – the result of some battle or other, I suppose. He got really angry and picked up one of the rower's oars with his good hand and gave the metal cable a couple of powerful blows while at the same time roaring: 'por los viente cuatro cocones de las doce aposteles!' ('by the power of the twenty-four testicles of the twelve apostles') – commanding the cable to move. The cable budged and the raft began to move and we reached the other side without any further delay. And I remember noting that Spanish lieutenant's sentence in my memory bank as we crossed over. There were lorries waiting for us and we were loaded aboard and set out for the field hospital straight away. The journey was very rough over jagged and broken roads. In the same lorry as me was a man on a stretcher who'd been badly injured in the stomach. To look at him, you'd have thought he was dead, he was that quiet and still. But any time the lorry shuddered or struck a rock and the road jolted him, he screamed out in pain. Eventually, we reached the field where the hospital had been set up around a series of tents. After a quick examination I was given an injection. Then, another journey to the train station, to the hospital in Mataró, which was about 20 miles north of Barcelona. They'd a special train laid on for the wounded – *el tren de los heridos* [the train of the wounded]. The view from the train was incredible – a stunning landscape and really beautiful countryside – along parts of the Costa Brava for example, but given the condition we were in, it would be an exaggeration to say that we enjoyed the journey as we should have. On reaching the station, at Mataró was a fleet of ambulances waiting for us and we were brought onto the hospital. Going through the hospital gate, I spotted a security man there dressed from head to toe in a brand-new uniform and Sam Browne belt and the thought struck me that – 'the further from battle, the better the soldier's kit'.

Before long, I was carried upstairs where I was put into bed number 34. It was a German doctor attending me. He was Jewish and a refugee from his own country. He took an x-ray of my injury and I asked him how long I'd have to stay in bed for. 'About two weeks,' the doctor said. 'Two weeks in bed!' 'That's bad enough', I thought to myself. They put my foot in plaster then. In the bed next to me on my left was an American who'd been wounded in the throat. He had a piece of shrapnel stuck close to his voice-box and could only speak in a whisper. The director of the hospital who was also Head Doctor came around one day on a hospital visit; he was American and looked very like Humphrey Bogart. On top of this, he even had the same mannerisms as Bogart as well. At one stage, he asks Gus Mikades[1] – the man with the injured throat – 'How do you feel?'

'I get headaches. I think that's because I read too much,' Gus whispers in reply. The doctor stared at him quietly for a moment. Then slowly and deliberately he says,' Listen – I'm the doctor here. You don't tell me what causes it. D'yeh get it?' Gus indicated that he'd 'got it!' The Spaniard to my right loved talking. He'd been wounded in the leg and even if his injury was quite a bad one, this hadn't interfered with his tongue at all. He never stopped yapping – even for a minute! Whenever he had visitors, you'd have thought that a dozen public meetings were going on at the same time, there was such a racket! Another man lying close to me had a wound that had gone septic and the blood and pus were seeping out through his big bloodstained bandage. The flies were buzzing around him. For a moment, I saw all the flies and midgets feeding drunkenly on the red wine back in the rocks again – in my imagination. Gradually, I got to know the nurses there. Most of them were Spaniards but there was also a Romanian woman, an American and Englishwoman in the ward. A Spanish nurse was looking after me for most of my time there in Mataró. Her name was Josefina and you couldn't have had a kinder or more warmhearted person as a nurse. The doctors did everything they could to try and reset the damaged bone in my foot but the wound went septic unfortunately, and despite their best efforts, they'd no choice but to amputate the foot in the end. Consequently, I can say in all honesty that I already have 'one foot in the grave!' There was no lift in the building and when anyone was being brought to the operating theatre the stretcher bearers had to manipulate the stretcher over the banisters on the stairs. After one operation I had – just before I woke up probably – (because they say that you can't have dreams while you're under anesthetic) I thought the truth had been revealed to me and I had a knowledge of all things – a sort of a 'revelation' so to speak.

'I understand the meaning of life,' I said to Carlos, the German doctor. 'What is it?' he said.

I thought for a moment but then had to admit – 'I'm not sure.'

'You've already forgotten,' he says laughing.

Another time I woke up and I was lying on my side on the operating table. A wide expanse of blue sky stretched away off into the distance – for as far as my eyes could see – through the hospital window, the whole world appeared quiet and dignified, and incredibly peaceful. The silence was broken suddenly by the sound of a man speaking German and the thought came to me right there and then – and I remember that it didn't surprise me one bit either – 'God is a German. What else!' These strange hallucinations only ever lasted couple of seconds, I suppose. Bill McGregor visited me one day. Apparently, he'd been slightly injured in an accident with a hand grenade. He told me that he'd looked on as an enemy plane was shot down just prior to crossing the Ebro again.[2] He'd some sad news to impart also. Frank Airlie had died on the ground-floor ward of the same hospital we were in. Bill and a number of other visitors had been chatting to Frank only the day before when he'd been sitting up in the bed with a big smile on his face – but tragically, he'd been found dead in bed the following next morning. I often remember Frank saying that he'd have been happy to have emerged from the war with his accent and his sexual organs unscathed. When Bill was returning to the Battalion he'd come over to say goodbye to me.

Little did I think then that he'd never see Ireland again and that an early death was all that lay ahead of him. A few months later he was killed along with many others in the terrible, interminable fighting that went on outside Gandesa. Harry Pollitt,[3] General Secretary of the Communist Party of Great Britain visited the hospital accompanied by Peter Kerrigan, correspondent with the *Daily Worker*. Peter was a tall straight-backed Scotsman. He was showing Harry around the place and looking after him well while he was on his visit. Someone attempted to delay them at one stage with some boring conversation or other but Peter interrupted him with – 'Harry is in a hurry now. He has a meeting that he's got to attend.' 'When I spotted you first, I thought you were Seán Murray,' says I. He laughed. 'Seán Murray thinks that he's better-looking than me,' he says with a laugh. An English nurse by the name of Barbara was looking after me the odd day.

'You have a lovely heart,' she says to me one morning.

I was delighted on hearing this, until I understood that she was referring to the fact that I had a strong and regular heartbeat. She was taking my pulse at the time! The American nurse was very unhappy with everyday working conditions in the hospital. She'd say, 'I'm a fully qualified nurse and I'm only wasting my time here. I'm always asking them to send me to the frontline of the fighting but they won't listen to me. I'm here, making beds instead!' Another American nurse joined us after a while and she'd the sort of face that you'd expect beneath a nun's habit, pale, cold and virginal. One day as she was doing her rounds, she overheard Josefina saying to me 'You're smoking a cigarette. That means you're on the mend.' The American gave her a cold stare – as she did me also. 'That doesn't mean anything,' she says, 'I've often seen someone smoking one minute and the next minute they're dead.' Having boosted my spirits in this way, she walked on haughtily to the next patient!

A low-sized Scotsman, a member of No. 1 Company, arrived in to talk to me one day. He'd been injured in the hand. After a short conversation, and just as he was leaving, he turns to me and says: 'I'm going downtown tonight. Do you want me to get you a bottle of wine?' I gave him the money and off he went. Later that night when everyone on the ward other than me was asleep, the Scotsman tiptoed slowly and quietly across the room to my bed. He left the bottle of wine on the bed and shoved the money I'd given back into my hand again. 'What's this?' I said. He didn't say anything but slipped away again as quietly as he'd appeared. He was no sooner gone out the door however but a Spanish man runs in and he's in a very agitated state altogether. 'Donde está mi botella de vino?'['Where's my bottle of wine?'], he bursts out at the top of his voice, running up and down the room and searching all the patients in their beds. He was absolutely livid. Needless, to say, I understood immediately what had happened and I stretched out and handed him the bottle of wine. He took it from me and left again immediately. He knew that I wasn't responsible for whatever shenanigans had gone on. By now everyone in the ward had woken up but they weren't long going back to sleep again. I actually spent the rest of that night deep in contemplation on that particular philosophical question – how can someone be so dishonest that they'd steal someone else's wine but at the same time be so honest that they'd hand all my money back to me again?

CHAPTER 7

WOE TO THE LOSER

An American used to call into me for a chat sometimes while I was in hospital. He couldn't extend his arm or hand and although his injury had healed, the muscles in his arm were still withered. They massaged his arm every day to try and strengthen it. 'Eh, Red?', he'd say, trying his best to straighten his arm but he could never manage it.

'I'll never be able to straighten this arm again,' he'd say. We heard in September that the government had decided to repatriate all foreigners from Spain. A few days later 'Popeye' – this was the American's nickname – appeared and walked over to my bed and says: 'Look!' He was able he stretch his arm out straight again.

'How did you manage that?', says I.

'Strength of will,' he said, and off he went again laughing quietly to himself.

Prior to hearing the announcement concerning the repatriation of foreign soldiers, it used to amaze me the number of men who'd arrive in the hospital with very minor injuries looking for treatment. Sam Wild had been very reluctant to leave the front when he was wounded in the hand because he didn't think his injury was bad enough to prevent him fulfilling his duties as a commander but he was given no choice in the matter. And when I heard this about Sam I had a feeling that the government had already decided to reduce the number of Brigade members at the front as quickly as possible and replace them with Spaniards. In this way it would make little difference militarily when the International Brigades were eventually withdrawn from the front.

There was a man in the hospital who'd received a minor injury in the fighting at the Ebro, had a nice 'artistic-looking' wound in the shoulder. This man had a habit of going around the place without any pajama jacket on him so that everybody could see the bandage wrapped around his torso and that covered only a very small wound. The way this man went on you'd swear he'd been cut in two and then sewn back together again.

Another man arrived into the hospital one day who'd received a promotion on the battlefield just shortly prior to being injured. He placed a sign at the top of his bed with the words 'Tienente [Lieutenant] Brown' written on it. This man was a real comedian. 'I wouldn't like people to think that I'd anything to do with the rest of this rabble here,' he'd say, laughing.

There was an Englishman on the ward who'd had both his arms broken in the fighting. His arms were in splints and he couldn't do anything for himself – even when he went to the toilet, he had to have someone helping him. Someone told me about the time he'd paid a visit to the local brothel in Mataró. He was drinking with other Brigade members and a number of prostitutes, when one of the whores gave him the eye. A few minutes later and he whispered to his friends in a delighted voice: 'Oh boys,' he says, on a high, 'I've got a jack!'

Himself and the whore got up to go upstairs and the whole company burst out laughing as they watched her help him climb the stairs slowly and carefully, his arms stretched out in front of him like some kind of dummy and the girl holding onto him in case he fell.

There was an Italian a few beds down from me and he played the mandolin regularly. He was a good musician and played sweet music on it. Once I improved a bit, he gave me a few lessons on the mandolin. In recompense, I taught him a tune or two – including 'The Irish Washerwoman'. I whistled it for him and he followed me on the mandolin. We had a singer on the ward also. One morning, I heard what I thought was a terrible moaning or caterwauling coming from somewhere outside the ward, a noise that continued for a long time. Initially, I thought it sounded like someone dying. Maybe someone was undergoing an operation without anaesthetic, I thought to myself. But it was actually this man singing some flamenco songs.

Because the Irishmen all spoke English we were referred to as *Ingléses*. Even in documents I discovered afterwards, I noticed that I was always referred to as *Inglés* (English), this without ever being questioned about it. Strange to say, while the Americans also spoke English, the Spaniards could distinguish between them and the rest of us and could tell that they weren't English. But they couldn't distinguish between the English, the Scots, the Welsh and the Irish. They were all *Ingléses* as far as they were concerned.

I had to stay in bed for a good while and it was through visitors that I heard any news about what was going on in the world outside. Bad news reached me that Paddy O'Sullivan had died after being badly wounded in one of the assaults on Gandesa. His company had been forced to retreat and they couldn't retrieve Paddy with all the murderous killing that the enemy were doing and so his body had been left out 'en tierre de nadie' [no-mans-land]. Once darkness fell the stretcher-bearers went out but they couldn't find his body.

Max Nash[1], the young man who'd performed the Cossack dance at the Wolfe Tone celebrations had also been killed. His body was found and he'd been badly wounded in the chest. When they found him he had an open bandage in his hand; he must have died before he'd a chance to apply it to the wound.

The Englishman Lieutenant Lewis Clive was dead.[2] From what I heard, he'd been pointing the enemy position out to the men in his company, and raised himself too high above the parapet momentarily. He'd barely finished speaking when he fell back amongst his own men, shot dead instantly by a sniper. As mentioned earlier, news reached us in September that the Spanish government was intent on repatriating all foreign fighters in the Brigades. On hearing this, the German doctor said sadly – 'You have place to go, yes? You are lucky.' The man had no country to return to; he'd been left stateless and displaced forever.

El Director, the American in charge of the hospital, spoke to his fellow-countryman Gus Mikades. Gus had to have a medical operation but it was a very dangerous one as a piece of shrapnel was caught near the main artery in his throat. 'We're happy enough to go ahead with the operation in the hospital here but the choice is yours. You'll be going home soon and you can wait till then if you wish.' Gus gave the operation some thought and decided that he stood a better chance at home and so he decided to wait until he was back in the United States.

'That's fine', says the Director. 'Take it easy in the meantime.' He gave Gus a look.

'Y' know what I mean?'

'I do.'

'Take it easy', the Director says again and walks away.

The Scotsman Cornwallis,[3] the machine-gunner, was sitting on the end of my bed one day. We were chatting away when out of the blue I asked: 'How's Jack Nalty anyway?' He gave me a shocked look. 'Nalty's dead,' he says.[4]

I must have been so shocked that I couldn't say anything. 'He was shot number of times at close range. He died three hours later.'

I couldn't understand it fully, a great wave of sadness passed through me on hearing this. Other people whom I knew had been killed and I was devastated on hearing of their deaths for some reason this was worse than any of them and I felt physically sick in a way that I'd never had before. We kept talking for another while but about other things and I didn't hear anything anymore.

From the stories coming out, and the news we heard every day about the slaughter, it wasn't difficult to imagine the horror of what was going on at the battlefront.[5] Bill McGregor himself was also dead. No wonder, Josefina asked me: '*Por que está tan triste Rubito?*' [Why are you so sad, Blondie?] One day as I hobbled around the place on my crutches, I called into the office down in the hospital yard, where the American Director of the hospital had his office. His desk was covered with official papers and documents and rubber stamps and a crowd of people sat around the room waiting to be served. A big fat man stood in front of the counter dressed in a very fine ceremonial-type uniform, a jacket sporting fancy ribbons and epaulettes and all the rest of it. This must be Miaja, the defender of Madrid, or someone really important, I thought.

Next thing, the Director writes something on a piece of paper and throws it on the counter in front of the big (and important, as I thought) man and says to him: 'Here's the pass – and don't fuck about now!')

'General Miaja' accepted the pass in humble fashion and went away again. It was obvious that the army's military authority and discipline was breaking down, slowly but surely. I was very relieved to find out afterwards that the man in the fancy uniform was only the head chef in the hospital and not a leading general! Josefina's mother paid a visit and was introduced to me. She had the same kind and generous nature as her daughter and I could tell that it wasn't from the wind that Josefina had taken her kindness, her kind and sweet personality. Her mother gave me a bottle of champagne as a present. I thought then – and I still think – it very funny that I tasted that drink – it always linked in my mind with the rich and bloated capitalists of this world – for the first time ever in the Spanish Republic, a place where even bread, the staple food of life, was fairly difficult to come by at the time.

One of the last memories I have of Mataró relates to the time the orchestra visited from Barcelona – the city orchestra – and played some light classical music for us patients. I stood on the balcony that evening watching the orchestra and listening to their pleasant music. To one side of me were a group of Americans playing darts and trying to put a spell on their flying darts by accompanying their throws with burps! On the other side of me was a nurse giving a tall, fat man a bath by emptying a bucket of water over him – a kind of a shower, you'd have called it, I suppose. The sight of this fat man reminded me for some reason of the time I'd seen Father McGrath from Saint Michael and John's Church after he'd been swimming in the Forty-Foot. While dressing himself, he'd been giving out stink to some other priests about 'the Spanish Reds.' He was a big fat man, the same as this man here in Spain. 'A circular priest' was what came to mind in that moment.

A Stint in S'Agaró

On the 22 October a number of us were transferred to S'Agaró. I missed the routines and voices I'd got used to even the barber who'd nicked me when he was shaving me and the American from Florida who'd sit on the side of my bed describing the size of the oranges they grew locally and boasting about what he got up to when he went to *la casa de putas* [brothel] and generally boasting endlessly about this, that and the other. S'Agaró was a beautiful area situated on the Costa Brava and the houses or villas where we were put up were right on the edge of the Mediterranean. We had an incredible view when we awoke every morning, the sea just a few steps away from us stretching out to the horizon – a view more beautiful and peaceful than anywhere else on earth. The villas were owned by rich people prior to the beginning of the war. They had that look about them too – a kind of a millionaire's row, that's for sure.

Maybe I'm confused now but I don't remember seeing any church at all in the area. The first building and the most obvious one that one noticed everywhere in Spain was the local church but in this place – the playground or pleasure-ground of the rich – there was none to be seen. As Peadar O'Donnell once said: 'There isn't an ounce of religion in an acre of millionaires.' When one considers the difficulties that the government had to overcome at this time, it's incredible really how good the care was that they provided for us. I received a regular massage to make sure the muscles and the sinews of my good foot got stronger and it was the same for the other men – whatever care they needed was given to them. Prior to leaving Mataró, I'd been given a card on which was noted every information relating to my injury and the treatment I needed for it.

There were nurses assigned to every villa – amongst them was Angela Guest, the sister of David who'd been killed at Gandesa.[6] She spoke fluent German, Spanish and French. Every facility and opportunity was provided us to ensure our time there passed as pleasantly as possible. We even had a sitting-room where we could read or write letters and play chess etc. Only one incident occurred that reminded us of the war during the entire time we were there. One day we spotted a ship a good distance offshore. Suddenly she altered course and began making for the shore at an incredible speed. It was amazing really how quickly she moved for such a big vessel. Initially, we couldn't understand the reason for this sudden change of course but then we spotted that a bomber plane had appeared in the sky and was pursuing the ship. With the bright gleam of sunshine on the plane's fuselage – you'd have thought the bomber was an innocent piece of silver on the horizon. Next thing a huge column of water shot up into the air right next to the ship and we heard the sound of gunfire and shelling. The bomber disappeared quickly again however and the ship resumed its normal course

We had a library with a nice mixture of books – enough to satisfy any reader's taste in literature – from *The Postman Always Rings Twice* to Proust. There was no lack of culture in S'Agaró either, that's for sure. Food was scarce however and as the American said, 'we've plenty of Shakespeare but not much bacon.'

We were well-used to going without food by this stage however. We knew that nothing could be done about the food shortages and that everyone was in the same boat. There was no shortage of music either. We organised a concert one night and amongst our musicians were a violinist and a double-bass player. The double-bass player was an Austrian and he was accompanied by the American nurse I mentioned earlier – the woman who'd been in the hospital in Mataró who'd had the look of a nun about her. She was fluttering around him and attending to his every need. I heard that they were just after getting married.

The first time I ever saw dubbed film was in a cinema in San Feiliu de Guixols, just a few miles from S'Agaro. An ambulance brought us from the hospital to the cinema one evening and while I can't remember the title of the film anymore, I know that Myrna Loy was the main actor in it. It was funny to watch the characters' mouths moving as if they were speaking English and the Spanish words coming out on the voice narration that accompanied the film. The place was crowded with young people making a big racket. It reminded me of the 'Mary-o' or the Lyceum back in Dublin.

I also loved sitting out in the garden of the villa, the Mediterranean stretched out before me, the sun shining and the smell of flowers in my nostrils, far away from the noise of the war. There are noises other than the sounds of war however. There was an American there who had a habit of asking me questions as if he was gathering information to write a thesis at some university or other when he was released from hospital. What influence did James Joyce have on Irish literature? – and other questions of this type. I was a great help to him. *En una palabra* [In one word] I'd reply, 'I don't know.'

He'd ask me then about Charlie Donnelly[7] as he was already well-known as a poet then – this despite the fact that he was quite young when he was killed at the Battle of Jarama earlier the previous year. I was able to provide him with a small bit of information about Charlie. Charlie Donnelly had often been in Connolly House during the early 1930s. I remember well training him in on how to work the printing machine there – it was one of those worked by a foot-pedal. We were producing pamphlets to hand out amongst the public. Charlie was working the foot pedal as quickly as he could one day when Seán Murray, the Party Secretary arrived in. He took up one of the pamphlets and read it. 'Are they all done?', he asks – it was obvious that something was bothering him. 'Most of them. Why? What's wrong?', says I. The pamphlets included a mantra of sorts at the bottom that said: FOR A WORKERS' REPUBLIC!

'That should read "FOR A WORKERS' AND SMALL FARMERS' REPUBLIC!"', says Seán. As the pamphlets were to be distributed amongst the working class in Dublin city myself and Charlie thought that Murray's suggestion was a bit over the top. To be honest, we both nearly burst out laughing but managed to keep a handle on ourselves. Anyway, the poor small farmers were left out on that occasion!

Charlie first showed an interest in politics when he was a student in University College Dublin. In 1934, he spent two weeks in Mountjoy. He was arrested and found guilty of involvement in an illegal picket outside the Somax shirt factory in South Great Georges Street.[8] The judge was happy to grant him bail, but Charlie wouldn't accept this and explained why he didn't want to be bailed. 'I would consider it more criminal in the circumstances to keep the peace than not to keep the peace.' The judge was horrified on hearing this response from him and told Charlie that he didn't really want to impose any penalty on him – neither a fine nor a prison sentence. He believed that he had someone of good standing before him – someone who had gone slightly over-the-top as regards their commitment to the cause etc.

But the judge couldn't get Charlie to change his mind. 'Fourteen days', he says in a patient voice in the end. Charlie eventually had to give up university because his father refused to pay his college fees unless he agreed to give up his political activities – something he was unwilling to do. Later that same year, 1934, his close friend Cora Hughes and May Laverty were locked up in Mountjoy for a while too. A poor tenant was about to be evicted from 28 York Street, a woman who had an income of 7/6 or 37½ pence a week of which she had to pay 10/- (50p) in rent. Her furniture was thrown out onto the street and Cora and May took it back in again. They received one month's imprisonment for this offence. Cora and Charlie were often together. Later, when he worked in London at a later stage, washing dishes in a hotel there, a man who worked with him told me that Charlie always kept a lock of Cora's hair amongst his possessions.

In 1935, the transport workers in Dublin went out on strike. The government (Fianna Fáil were in power at the time) announced that they'd arranged for army lorries to be put on the streets in order to provide a transport service for the people of the city. In response to the government's statement the IRA said that they were siding with the strikers. Charlie was very agitated about this turn of events at the time as there was a chance that civil war might erupt if the government interfered in this manner. In the end, the government went ahead and put military lorries on the streets and the IRA made no attempt to prevent this. While he was no fanatic from a nationalist point of view, when the British battalion was set up in Spain at the end of January 1937, Charlie chose to join the Americans instead. When I first met David Guest in Spain, he reminded me of Charlie. Both men were intellectuals who looked more natural with a book under their arm than a rifle on their shoulder. I met an Irish-Canadian in S'Agaró who'd been born in Belfast but whose family had emigrated to Canada when he was very young. He'd lost a hand in the battle of Ypres but it always amazed me how quickly and efficiently he could roll cigarettes with his one good hand. There was also an American there named Paul whose foot was in plaster. Whenever you heard 'CLUMP, CLUMP, CLUMP' behind you, you could be sure Paul was on his way. He was always singing 'Why Build a Wall round a Graveyard when Nobody Wants to go in':

> They always build fences around gardens, of course,
> To keep people out I agree,
> They always build walls round a prison because
> If they didn't well – where would they be?
> With that there is nothing amiss,
> But will you please tell me this –
> Why build a wall round a graveyard, etc.

I noticed around this time also how quickly American terminology was adopted by other nationalities. 'Radio' instead of 'wireless' (the usual term used in the 1930s), 'mail' instead of 'post' etc. As for the common-held view that specific traits can be ascribed to particular nationalities[9] – even if one can go too far with such generalisations – there is some truth in them all the same. The Americans were inclined to be loudly spoken and forceful at times while the Germans could be dour and stoic as compared with the Italians. One evening Bill McGregor told a crowd of us in Marçà about an Irishman who was in Paris one night when they were on their way to Spain. They went into a bar and as it happens, the Irishman was the first person in the door. He came back out the door again as quickly as he'd gone in – and in an alarmed voice, he warned the others 'Don't go in there! Don't go in there! There's a naked woman in there – a naked woman!' While it might seem stereotypical, it is difficult to imagine anyone other than an Irishman acting like this during the 1930s! I myself was quite the innocent also. I was relaxing out in the garden one day when an American close by was examining a black line or mark on his foot.

'What caused that,' I ask.

'That was syph,' he says.

'What's syph?,' says I, and he shouts over to another American, 'Hey, Hank! There's a guy here wants to know what's syph!'

We had a gramophone in the villa, but similar to Paul, it only played the one tune – a German record with the song 'Freiheit' (Freedom). If we heard that song once we must have heard it a thousand times. In the library was a book by P.G. Wodehouse. I'd never enjoyed reading this particular author but because Peadar O'Donnell had made a laudatory reference to him in his book – *The Gates Flew Open*, I tried to read Woodhouse again but unfortunately, I still didn't get any enjoyment out of it.

In the library also, a young German man sat slouched over in an armchair every day, coughing miserably. He couldn't stop coughing, the poor man. He was suffering from tuberculosis. Looking across at me one day he said, in sad voice: 'I'd prefer to be like you and have just one foot than to have this awful disease.' It was at this juncture that the battle of the Ebro was being fought and, slowly but surely, Franco was getting the upper-hand. And, sure enough, one day in November I was reading *Mundo Obrero* and the bad news was right there on the very front page. The Republican Army had returned back across the Ebro again. Despite our initial progress and all the sacrifices made, our victory was as the sun that appears briefly to drive away the dark clouds. In reality, it was just the last throw of the dice.

Making for Home

Rumours had been circulating for a while and it wasn't long before they were confirmed. We were going home. We were put on the train back to France but on arrival at the border, the authorities would only allow their own citizens into France. A dispute arose and the Frenchmen who'd fought with the Brigades decided to return to S'Agaró with us in protest at this decision by the French government. After some discussions, we agreed it best however that if they went ahead and crossed into France where they could initiate a protest about our treatment within France itself. The rest of us returned to S'Agaró to wait another while for repatriation. What happened in France I'm not sure, but within a short time we were back on the move again. As it turns out, a group of nurses travelled in addition to ourselves on the next train we took back to France and who did I meet on the train but the Spanish nurse Josefina. A surge of joy went through me on seeing her again. I tried my best to say something romantic to her: 'Tu cara es siempre antes mis ojos,' [Your face is always before my eyes], I said but all she did was laugh. Maybe she thought her Irish was better than my Spanish! This time, the train stopped at a small train station somewhere near the border where André Marty give a speech from the platform. He spoke in French. Marty was an important and well-known figure in the Brigades but that was my first time ever seeing him in the flesh. He had a reputation for being a scary and intimidating character but I'm happy to say that he did nothing to scare Frank Ryan in any way. Ryan and himself had had a bit of an argument one day early on during the war, as a result of which he'd locked Frank up for a while; he'd had no choice but to release him again very shortly afterwards, needless to say.

This time the train continued its journey across the border and next thing we were in France. At one of the stops an American bought a box of matches. He promptly lit a match and watched it burn down to the root, then flicked it onto the ground. 'Good old capitalism', he said. It was on this same platform, just a short distance from Spain, that I had to say goodbye to Josefina. It was here also that I had to say my official farewell to *La Niña Bonita* – the poetic name for the Spanish Republic, (as Michael Lehane would have put it.) And now that the same Republic was in its death-throes, the French authorities did their best to get rid of us as quickly as they possibly could. Before long, we found ourselves on the boat to England. I can still see it now even all these years later – Tom Murphy (he lost an arm at Gandesa) standing at the bar on the boat, holding a glass of beer in his one good hand. On arrival in London we went to a hotel for a meal. The restaurant was upstairs on the first floor of the hotel where I watched as Tudor-Hart, the Englishman who'd been Head Surgeon in the hospital at Mataró, carried a very badly-injured man up the stairs. The next day 'Johnny' [James] Larmour, who was still working in the office in London, brought me to one of the hospitals by taxi for a medical exam.

'Is that stupidity still going on in Spain?', says the doctor, sarcastically.

'It is and it won't be long now before Hitler's ready and the same stupidity will be going on here', says 'Johnny' in reply. 'You might be right,' the doctor says laughing.

Then, we Irish went to the office of the Irish High Commissioner, Mr. Dulanty, in Regent Street. We sat waiting in the reception while a young clerk gave us dirty looks from behind the counter.

'Franco's winning,' he says after a while in an ignorant and accusatory way. This was the first insult we'd heard from anyone since our return. We didn't dignify his words with a response even if the thought went through my mind that this lad had a lot of potential for a career in the diplomatic service. Another functionary from the office accompanied us to Euston Station to make sure we got the train okay. We were on the final leg of her journey home. Jim Prendergast was waiting for us in Dún Laoghaire and was in the same carriage as myself and Michael Lehane on the train into the city. 'My advice to you was to keep your head down', he says, 'but I never thought of your leg!' 'Well,' I says, 'I can do without my foot but I definitely can't do without my head.' It was nearly Christmas time. Exiting the station at Westland Row I heard 'Silent Night' coming from a church close by and the rattle of collection boxes. We were back in the Isle of Saints and Scholars again, the country 'where to fail is more than to triumph and victory less than defeat.'

Seán Murray paid me a visit one night and it was obvious to me that he'd been really affected by the war – so many men had been killed and were dead and buried now – men that he'd always had a great fondness and respect for. On top of this, that really fine man Frank Ryan was now a prisoner-of-war and there was no hope at all left that the Spanish Republic would win the war.

'I can still read that newspaper,' I said to Seán, referring to the eye test he'd given me before I'd left for Spain that first day. This 'crack' got a laugh out of him.

The news from Spain got worse every day. On 23 December 1938, Franco began his final assault on Catalonia – the death-blow. The tragic dates followed one after another. Come 17 January, Tarragona was taken by enemy forces. On 26 January, Franco took over Barcelona. When I read the names of the towns I knew – even if I knew only a few of them – it was like being stabbed in the heart: Mataró, Cervera, Olot, Figueras…

The final meeting of the Cortes (the Spanish parliament) took place in Figueras in Castillo de San Fernando on 1 February 1939. By then almost half-a-million people had fled across the border to France, to escape the victors. By the end of March, the military part of the war was over.

This is a true and picture – warts and all – of what happened to me from when I left Dublin in March 1938 until my return again in December of the same year. I'm not claiming to give the full story of the British Battalion in this book. I can't remember everything after so many years but I can say with all honestly that whatever mistakes I may have made in this account, there are certainly no lies in it. All I have left now are *recuerdos* [memories] and a few small pieces of paper[10] such as the following: (Translated from Spanish by BM):

1. Military pay-book of Eugene Downing, 15th International Brigade, 57th Battalion, 4th Company, 35th Division. Infantry.
2. Account of his illness in medical terms.
3. Document from Don Antonio Cordón García, Sub-Secretariat of the Land Army of the Ministry of National Defence, stating that Eugene Downing had received wounds fighting at the front against the enemy and was now returning home.
4. Document from Dr. Sidney Vogel, Director of Blood Hospital No. 1, Mataró, date 22.10.1938.
5. Note from the Chief of the Central Administration of the International Brigades and of the Spanish Aid Committee in Dublin that Donnings [sic] Eugene was returning home for reasons of the withdrawal [of the brigades].
6. Letter from Union de Muchachas Espanolas with a multi-coloured ribbon – red, yellow and purple. The handwritten text:
   In the ultimate homage which the people can render to those who gave everything to our cause, we, the young women of Spain, make the firm promise that we shall work without wavering in order to create as soon as possible a country free of foreign invaders.
7. A piece of paper from the Bank of Spain, authorizing Eugene Donning [sic] to have 250 French francs in order to leave Spain./Inspector, 15.12.1938.

I received a letter from Josefina[11] one day in the post. Stamped on the cover were the words 'CENSURA MILITAR – BARCELONA'. On the edge of the envelope was the sentence 'Salud a Franco! Arriba Espana!', while at the top of the letter itself were the words 'Año de la Victoria'. The Republic was dead without a shadow of a doubt.

I began reading – *Mi querido Rubito…*

Notes

The Irish in the International Brigades: An Introduction

1. Esmond Romilly's *Boadilla* (London, 1971) is a classic account of the Madrid battles.
2. Richard Baxell, *Unlikely Warriors: The British in the Spanish Civil War and the Struggle against Fascism* (London, 2012).
3. Michael O'Riordan, *Connolly Column: The Story of the Irishmen who Fought in the Ranks of the International Brigades in the National-Revolutionary War of the Spanish People 1936–1939* (Dublin, 1979); Seán Cronin, *Frank Ryan: The Search for the Republic* (Dublin, 1980).

Chapter 1: Some Reflections on Ireland

1. Another slightly different version of that rhyme went as follows: *Plainy, clappy, rolley, to backey, Hippy, tippy, a jelly bag and basket.* (MOH)
2. I never thought back then that many years later, I'd find myself one sunny day in Keats House, Keats Grove, Hampstead, examining a plum tree respectfully, with a sign next to it in capital letters: '*THIS PLUM TREE REPLACES THE ONE BENEATH WHICH JOHN KEATS WROTE "ODE TO A NIGHTINGALE"*' (ED)

3. James Larkin Jnr (1904–69) was an Irish Labour Party politician and trade union official. He first stood for election as an *Irish Worker League* candidate at the September 1927 General Election for the Dublin County constituency but was unsuccessful. His father, James Larkin Snr, was a successful candidate for the Dublin North constituency at the same general election. The younger Larkin stood for the *Revolutionary Workers' Groups* in the 1930 Dublin City Council elections and was elected. He had attended the International Lenin School in Moscow in the years 1928–30. On the foundation of the Communist Party of Ireland in 1933, Larkin became its chairman. He was first elected to *Dáil Éireann* (Irish Parliament) as a Labour Party TD for the Dublin South constituency at the 1943 General Election and was re-elected at the 1944 General Election for the same constituency. He later moved to the Dublin South-Central constituency and was elected at both the 1951 and 1954 General Elections. (MOH, BM)
4. Born in Watford, England, Ruby Mildred Ayres (1881–1955) was a British love story writer and one of the most popular and prolific romantic novelists of the twentieth century. Some people have cited her as the inspiration for the P. G. Wodehouse character Rosie M. Banks. Several of her works became films and she did screenwriting for *Society for Sale* among others. (MOH)
5. Born into poverty and illegitimacy, Londoner Richard Horatio Edgar Wallace (1875–1932) was a well known and incredibly prolific English writer. He left school at the age of 12 and joined the British Army 9 years later where he worked as war correspondent during the Second Boer War, for both Reuters and the *Daily Mail*. Wallace wrote screenplays, poetry, historical non-fiction, 18 stage plays, 957 short stories, and over 170 novels. More than 160 films have been made of his work and one of his best remembered creations is *King Kong*. One of the most prolific thriller writers of the twentieth century, more than 50 million copies of Wallace's combined works were sold in various editions over the course of a few decades. (MOH)
6. *Seosamh Mac Grianna* (1900–90) was an Irish writer who was born into a family of poets and storytellers in Rann na Feirste (Ranafast) in the Donegal Gaeltacht. He is the most high-profile modern writer in Ulster Irish and considered one of the best Irish-language writers of the twentieth century. He trained as a teacher in St Patrick's College, Dublin, from which he graduated in 1921. He was involved in both the Irish War of Independence and the Civil War and was among a large group of Republicans interned by pro-Treaty Free State forces during the latter. Mac Grianna began writing in the early 1920s but his creative period was relatively short lasting, some 15 years or so. In 1935 he was stricken

by a severe depressive psychosis and admitted himself to a psychiatric hospital where he remained for many years. He is best known for his autobiography *Mo Bhealach Féin,* first published in 1940. (MOH)

7. The International Lenin School (ILS) was founded in 1926 as an instrument for the "'Bolshevisation'" of the Communist International (Comintern) and its national sections in various countries. It was closed in 1938. Students sent to the International Lenin School were handpicked by the Communist Parties of different countries, and four languages were used by the participants: Russian, German, English, and French. (MOH, BM)

8. Elizabeth 'Betty' Sinclair (1910–81) was a communist activist who was born into a working-class Church of Ireland family from the Ardoyne area of Belfast in Northern Ireland. While in her early twenties, she joined the Revolutionary Workers' Group (RWG) and was involved in the Outdoor Relief Strike of 1932 after which she attended the International Lenin School in Moscow. She took part in a number of elections and was appointed full-time secretary of the Belfast and District Trades Union Council and was the Council's representative at the talks which founded the Northern Ireland Civil Rights Association (NICRA) in 1967. Sinclair served as NICRA chairperson for 2 years but resigned in 1969 claiming the organisation had become dominated by ultra-leftists and was aggravating sectarian divisions as a consequence. In 1975, she moved to Prague where she worked for the *World Marxist Review* for a number of years. She died in east Belfast in 1981. (MOH)

9. In July 1939 Ewart Milne, Jim Prendergast, Michael Waters and I visited the House of Commons in Westminster to speak to Ellen Wilkinson one of the leaders of the Labour Party about the campaign being organised by the 'Release Frank Ryan Committee.' When Ellen Wilkinson arrived to meet us, it was clear from her rushed demeanor that she was as good as saying to us – 'I have more important things to be doing then this'; that we weren't welcome there. She had some document or other in her hand and said that she was in a big hurry. We explained to her that all we were requesting was that she ask a question in the House about Frank. She wouldn't do this, however. 'It would be like a red rag to a bull for me to raise such a matter with a Tory government. Get someone else.' We were very disappointed at this. Needless to say, the Spanish Republic was a dead dream at this stage – and there was nothing to be gained with this issue – and as a politician, she was just jettisoning a lost cause. On another occasion following this, a deputation visited the Spanish ambassador in London to register their unhappiness at the continued imprisonment of Frank Ryan in Spain, despite the fact that the war was over. He was a prisoner-of-war the deputation argued and should have been freed.

The deputation had a list of names and organisations that were appealing for Frank's release and they presented this to the ambassador. The Duke of Alba accepted the list enthusiastically – 'I'm always happy', he said laughing, 'to receive lists such as this so that I can study them and then file them away.' Edward Milne was involved with a medical facility in Spain during the war and achieved fame as a poet. In the years following the Spanish Civil War, he changed his political perspective on those events, and in 1978, I received a letter from him saying, 'Incidentally, my own politics have swung right around and today I'm more or less conservative. Like Auden, I think most of my writing of those late Thirties and Forties was very misguided.' And in another letter from him: 'I certainly repent my mistaken attitude in the Thirties, just as Robert Conquest, or Paul Johnson, or for that matter, old Wordsworth did in the past, or as Auden did in the not so distant past.' Based on this reference to Wordsworth, it appears that not only was he opposed to the Soviet Union but also the French Revolution. (ED)

10. The first of the Animal Gangs is believed to have originated in a dispute between the IRA and a group of young newspaper sellers from Corporation Buildings and surrounding areas. A crisis emerged in September and October 1934, when a printers' strike meant that the boys who sold newspapers were left entirely reliant on sales of the Irish Republican newspaper 'An Phoblacht'. Worried by their plummeting income, the newspaper-sellers demanded a better price from the IRA for selling the newspaper, a demand which was refused. The dispute turned violent and a savage street brawl took place. The IRA viewed the brawl as an affront to its authority and a number of violent incidents and tit-for-tat assaults and attacks occurred. The IRA harassed the newspaper-sellers and targeted the dance halls these youths frequented, and the violence spilled out onto the streets before eventually petering out after a couple of weeks. Such was the savagery with which the newspaper-sellers fought their ground however that high-ranking IRA member Frank Ryan described them as little better than animals at one point. The sobriquet that was the 'animal gangs' was born. The gangs were believed to have had their base primarily in and around the Liberties and Foley Street areas of the city, and were involved protection rackets, providing muscle as enforcers and other petty criminal activities. (MOH)

11. The dispute centred on the sacking of Ryan's comrade Frank Edwards, a primary school teacher at Mount Sion, Waterford, by Bishop Kinane in 1935. The dismissal was due to agitation against slum-landlords and Edwards's membership of the Republican Congress, the organisation that Ryan had co-founded. Edwards was later a Communist and fought in the International Brigades. (BM)

12. In 1941, Bernard McGinn's play *Remembered Forever* was produced in the Abbey Theatre – a cynical play about 1916. Seán McEntee criticised the play as an insult to the heroes of the Easter Rising. (ED)

13. 'Two young Dublin men, Paddy Kevin Blake of Hardwicke Street and Paddy Cochrane, who are members of the British Medical Unit, serving with the Government forces in Spain, had an amazing escape from death after the fighting in Belchite. They are now convalescing in Valencia, having practically recovered from their wounds. Blake had been fighting with the Government forces in Spain since the outbreak of the war. On April 3 he was wounded and after some months he rejoined and took up duty with the British Medical Unit. It appears that the night before Belchite was taken, Blake and Cochrane were in the town looking for abandoned enemy lorries, ambulances, or other motor vehicles, when an Insurgent, hiding in a nearby house, hurled a hand-grenade at them. The grenade dropped right between them, exploded, and sprayed them with shrapnel. Cochrane was the more seriously injured of the two, in the leg. Together they managed to get into an empty house nearby and Blake, who was able to walk, later elected to set out to get help for his comrade. Leaving his companion in the house he set off to see if he could find some of the Government soldiers. It was learned last night that Blake has been complimented by the Spanish Government for his heroic and courageous act and has been promoted to a high rank in the unit in which he is serving.' (*The Irish Press*, 6 Oct. 1937). (ED)

14. Cora Hughes died on the 18 April 1940 in her parents' house in Dublin and was buried in Killure Graveyard in Coillte Mach (Kiltimagh), County Mayo. Born in Kiltimagh originally, she'd been educated at the Saint Louis Convent there after which she completed a BA and an MA in Celtic Studies at University College Dublin. At one stage she was the treasurer of the Thomas Davis branch of the Gaelic League. Her health failed her as a consequence of all the work she did amongst the Dublin poor, and she was just 27 years of age when she died. When I visited the graveyard in Killure in 1982 I couldn't locate her grave. (ED)

15. *Scéala Éireann* (English: *The Irish Press*) was an Irish national daily newspaper published by Irish Press PLC between 5 September 1931 and 25 May 1995. (MOH)

16. Here's an excerpt from the *Connacht Tribune* dated 27 of April 1940: 'A SPANISH WARRIOR. At a meeting of the Mayo Board of Health a letter was received from Thomas McMullen, Westport Quay, requesting to be furnished with straps for his artificial limb. He mentioned that he lost his leg while fighting with the anti-communist forces in Spain. As he was only a volunteer General Franco had no money to pension him ... The Board decided to grant the application.' The report never mentioned whether bishops in Ireland made any effort to save this poor man from public embarrassment but heartlessly left him reliant on charity instead. Similar to the Irish who fought on behalf of the Pope against Garibaldi these recruits were consigned to the rubbish bin of history. (ED)

17. Ernst Toller (1893–1939) was a German Expressionist poet and playwright. As a leading member of the Independent Social Democratic Party of Germany (USPD), Toller took part in the short-lived Bavarian Soviet Republic in 1919 and later spent four years in prison. During the Weimar Republic Toller wrote plays, poetry and a biography of his youth. He fled from the Nazis to Switzerland in 1933. In May 1939, six weeks after Franco seized Madrid, Ernest Toller hanged himself in the Mayflower Hotel in New York. It was said that he wore himself out with work and that he was depressed at the collapse of the Republic. He was 46 years of age. (ED, BM)

18. James (Jim) Gralton (1886–1945) was an Irish socialist leader. Born in April, 1886, in Effrinagh, County Leitrim, Gralton was one of seven children and grew up on a small farm there. Gralton emigrated to the US in 1909 and became a US citizen but returned to Ireland to fight in the Irish War of Independence and later again, in 1932, to look after his mother, when he also led the Revolutionary Workers' Group in Leitrim, a precursor of the Communist Party of Ireland. He ran a dance hall in Effrinagh, where he organised free events at which he expounded his political views. There were violent protests against these dances, led by a number of Catholic clergy which culminated in a shooting incident staged by the local IRA. Shortly after this incident, on the 9 February 1933, Gralton was arrested, and later deported to the US, on the basis that he was considered an 'alien' in Ireland at this point. This led to public protests. Jim Gralton died in New York on 29 December 1945. In 2014, a film entitled *Jimmy's Hall*, based on Jim Gralton's life and telling the story of his deportation to the United

States in 1933, appeared in cinemas worldwide. The film was directed by well-known British film-maker Ken Loach. (MOH, BM)

Chapter 2: The Journey to Spain

1. According to an essay written by Hywel Francis, University College of Swansea, titled 'A study of Welsh miners in the Spanish Civil War', as published in the *Journal of Contemporary History*, 1970, vol. 5, 118 miners from Wales took part in the Spanish Civil War. (ED)
2. Not identified. Either the man enlisted under a different identity or Eugene got his name wrong. (BM)

Chapter 3: Barcelona

1. William Bibby was from Birkenhead, single, and an electrician. He was wounded on the Ebro, 27 July 1938. (BM)
2. Probably James Cunningham from Glasgow, who joined the British battalion on 30 March 1938 and was killed on the Ebro, 28 July 1938. (BM)
3. Airlie was mortally wounded on the Ebro, July 1938. (BM)
4. I saw a photo of this occasion. The clock of City Hall shows that it was two minutes past two. After the Republic was crushed, Lluis Companys was arrested in France in 1940. Marshal Petain sent him to back to Franco. He was executed in Monjuich Prison Barcelona on 15 October 1940 and *Visca Cataluna* (Catalonia Forever) – as his last words. (ED)

Chapter 4: Through Catalonia

1. John Longstaff from Stockton-on-Tees was 18 when he joined the Brigades in September 1937. He survived the war (BM).
2. A line from the famous Irish ballad 'The Wild Rover.' (MOH)
3. Boswell was a single man from Coventry, an actor and a shop-steward in an aircraft factory. He was killed on the Ebro, 28 July 1938. (BM)
4. Baile na hAbhann is a Gaeltacht village and townland about 30 kilometres west of Galway, Ireland, on the road between Indreabhán and Casla. In English, Baile na hAbhann means 'river settlement'. (MOH)
5. James Glavin, 39 years old, was a married man from Glasgow. Glavin was sent to the disciplinary squad because of drinking. Re-joined the British battalion on 15 August and was wounded two days later. Ex-British Army. (BM)
6. Not identified.
7. *Kai Lung Unrolls His Mat* is a fantasy novel by English writer Ernest Bramah. First published in 1928, it has been reprinted a number of times in the decades since. Ernest Bramah (1868–1942) was an English author who published 21 books and numerous short stories and features. Highly-regarded in his day, he wrote humorous works, detective stories and supernatural stories. George Orwell acknowledged that Bramah's book, *What Might Have Been,* influenced his *Nineteen Eighty-Four.* Unrolling his mat is something a central character of Bramah's – the character known as Kai Lung does often (usually in the shade of a mulberry tree), before relating stories about his various adventures.(MOH)
8. During the Second World War at one stage, after Russia had become involved, I met Paddy O'Daire at a party in London. He was in the British Army. Another Irishman says to him: 'I never thought I'd see you in the King's uniform!' Paddy looked at him and says: 'This uniform is a sign that I'm a good Marxist.' (ED)
9. Frank Proctor, b. 1915, from Liverpool, was a fitter and joined the Brigades in May 1937. A Sergeant, he first served in the anti-tank battery. He was mortally wounded in the head by a shell splinter in the Sierra Pandols on 24 August 1938 and he died on his way to hospital. (BM)

10. Probably David Anderson from Aberdeen , ex-Gordon Highlander, went to Spain in February 1937, later instructor. Wounded in the arm on the Ebro on 27 July 1938, Anderson left Spain as a stowaway. (BM)

11. Probably John Dunlop, an apprentice chartered accountant from Glasgow who survived the war. (BM)

12. Lewis Clive (1910 –1938) was the son of Lt.-Col. Percy Clive, a Liberal Unionist and later a Conservative MP for Ross who was killed during the First World War. Clive attended Oxford and rowed in the Boat Races, during both 1930 and 1931. He won a gold medal in coxless pairs at the 1932 Olympics. Clive was commissioned in the Grenadier Guards Reserve but resigned his commission five years later. A member of the Fabian Society, Clive was involved in local politics and was elected as a Labour Councillor in the borough of Kensington. He joined the International Brigade in February 1937. He was a company commander in the British Battalion of the IB but was killed in action at Hill 481, near Gandesa, 1 August 1938. (MOH, BM)

13. 'You're My Heart's Desire, I Love You, Nellie Dean' is a sentimental ballad in common time by Henry W. Armstrong. First published in 1905, in New York, it was taken up in 1907 by the British music hall singer Gertie Gitana and became her most famous song. It was later very popular in the UK as a pub song, particularly the chorus 'There's an old mill by the stream, Nellie Dean...', which was often sung by itself. (MOH)

14. Bernard Burwell from Yorkshire was 23 when he went to Spain in 1938. He was wounded on the Ebro, 26 July 1938. (BM)

15. Ernest Gébler (1914–1998), sometimes known as Ernie Gébler, was an Irish writer of Czech origin. Gébler was born in Dublin, one of five children. His father was a shopkeeper and a musician of Czech-Jewish origin and his mother was a Dublin theatre usherette. During the 1930s Ernest worked backstage in the Gate Theatre. He was married twice, first to Leatrice Gilbert, daughter of the actors John Gilbert and Leatrice Joy, whom he met on a trip to Hollywood. The couple moved to Ireland, got married and had a son John Karl but divorced in 1952. Both mother and baby returned to America. Gébler met future novelist Edna O'Brien, then working in a pharmacist's shop in Dublin and, despite opposition from O'Brien's family, they moved to England and married in 1954. They had two sons, Karl (later Carlo), who is a well-known writer in his own right, and Sasha, an architect. O'Brien and Gébler separated in 1964 and divorced in 1968 with O'Brien eventually getting sole custody of the children. Gébler returned to live in Dublin in 1970 where he died in 1998 (MOH).

16. Michael Economides was born in Nicosia, Cyprus, in 1910. He arrived in Spain in early December 1936, where he joined the Marseillaise Battalion, 14th International Brigade. He fought at both Lopera and Las Rozas after which he joined British Battalion and was appointed Political Commissar at Tarazona de La Mancha training base. He was wounded in the leg at Jarama in February, 1937. He also took part in the Ebro Offensive where he was wounded in the chest, subsequent to which he was repatriated. He died in 1996. (MOH)

17. Robert Cooney was born in Sunderland in 1907 but his family moved to Aberdeen, Scotland while he was still a child. He attended the International Lenin School in Moscow 1931-32. He held a series of important positions in the British Battalion including those of Company Commissar, Brigade Adjutant Commissar and Battalion Commissar and saw action at Teruel, Seguera de los Baños, Caspe, Gandesa and during the Ebro Campaign between July and September 1938. He was repatriated in December, 1938. (MOH)

18. Jawaharlal Nehru referred to this visit in an article he published in the *National Herald* (Lucknow), 7 July 1939: 'Something in me wanted to stay on this inhospitable looking hillside which sheltered so much human courage, so much of what was worthwhile in life.' (ED)

19. David Haden Guest was born in 1911 London. He went to Cambridge University where he studied Maths, Philosophy and Economics. Working initially as an organiser with the YCL (Young Communist League) and as a lecturer at Marx House, he became a Mathematics lecturer at Cambridge University. In March, 1938, he arrived in Spain. He joined the British Battalion in May 1938 and participated in the Battle of the Ebro where he was killed by a sniper's bullet at Hill 481, 26 July 1938, during the Ebro battle. His sister Angela worked as a nurse in Spain. (MOH, BM)

CHAPTER 5: TO THE EBRO

1. From Shakespeare's *Cymbeline*, Act 3, Scene 6, uttered by Belarius, in the play about Ancient Britain. (BM)

2. Whenever this date falls on a Sunday, pilgrims who go to Santiago de Compostela, the main town in Galicia, receive a special dispensation. This occurred in 1937. For the sake of Franco's soldiers (other than the Moors, I suppose) who were unable to go on pilgrimage because of the war, the Pope granted an extension for the dispensation until 25 July 1938. (ED)

3. Charles L. Hart: aka 'Yorkie' was 25 years of age and from Leeds. He arrived in Spain on 14 January 1937. He served with the medical services as a driver and was repatriated sometime in 1938. (MOH, BM)

4. This is a pun on a line from the English-language version of the Irish national anthem 'The Soldier's Song' ('Amhrán na bhFiann' in Irish), the Irish national anthem, the original English lyrics and music of which was composed by Peadar Kearney sometime in late 1909 or early 1910. (MOH)

CHAPTER 6: AS A HOSPITAL PATIENT

1. Constantine Mikades was wounded during the defense of Hill 666 in the Sierra Pandols, receiving shrapnel in his neck he spent the remainder of his time in Spain in the hospital. (BM) Gus Mikades returned to America around about the 15 December 1938 on the French liner *Paris*. Unfortunately, he died while undergoing an operation in Beth Israel Hospital, New York on the 11 January 1939. He is buried in Long Island, New York. (ED)

2. In the book, *La guerra de Espana desde el aire* by Jesus Salas Larrazabal, it states that Heraclio Gautier Larrainzar was killed on the 20 July 1938 by a bullet to the side. He was flying low in a Fiat aircraft to examine the battleground when he was killed by small arms fire. Maybe this was the incident that Liam (Bill) McGregor witnessed. As for the letters that Bill sent home to his mother during the Battle of the Ebro here are some excerpts from them:

> *August 10 1938: I have been made political commissar of the Major Attlee Company. Previously, I was deputy-commisar of the machine-gun company where Jack Nalty is commander. In this company (the Major Attlee Co.) Paddy O'Daire is O.C. In fact, out of four companies, three commanders and one commissar are Irish. Paddy Duff is adjutant of the machine-gunners. August 16: Last night we captured a lot of Moors and rifles and other equipment - including a number of new British Hotchkiss guns. Such is 'non-intervention!'* (ED)

3. On Sunday, 3 September 1939, it was declared that war had broken out between Britain and Germany. Harry Pollitt issued a pamphlet entitled *How to Win the War* outlining the policy of the Communist Party of Great Britain in relation to the war and the reasons the party supported it. He emphasized the anti-fascist aspect of the war, as opposed to the British and French imperialism. As he said in the pamphlet: *The prosecution of this war necessitates a struggle on two fronts. First to secure the military victory over fascism and second, to achieve this, the political victory over the enemies of democracy in Britain.* On the 14 September, the *Communist International* declared from Moscow that: *'This war is an imperialist and predatory war.... an out and out imperialist war to which the working class in no country could give any support.'*

Both stances were in direct contradiction of one another. The party later changed its policy and opposed the war citing it as an imperialist war. Harry Pollitt was removed from his position as secretary-general and demoted. When the war began against the USSR (June 1941) the Party supported it as an anti-fascist war and Harry Pollitt was reinstated in his job as secretary-general. In 1946, Stalin stated that 'the second world war from the very outset assumed the nature of an anti-fascist war, a war of liberation, one of the tests of which was to re-establish democratic liberties.' It appears therefore that the Communist International had gone astray and that Harry Pollitt had pursued the correct policy from the very beginning. (ED)

CHAPTER 7: WOE TO THE LOSER

1. Max Nash was born in London in 1917 and worked as a commercial traveller. He was a member of the Young Communist League and went to Spain in October 1937. Nash was killed in one of the futile attempts to capture Hill 481 near Gandesa in July 1938. (BM)

2. Just a few months before Lewis Clive died, his book *The People's Army* was published in London. (ED)

3. George Cornwallis lived in London before he arrived in Spain in September 1937. A sergeant, Cornwallis was wounded at Caspe in March 1938 and again on the Ebro, 23 September 1938, the last day of combat. (BM)

4. Jack Nalty's sister spoke to Father Michael O'Flanagan when the bad news came through that Jack had been killed. She was a very devout person and consequently very worried about Jack's spiritual state and whether he could be in a State of Grace, given that he was fighting for the *Reds*. What would happen to him in the next life and so on. Father O'Flanagan told her not to worry in the slightest about it. Anyone who had given their life fighting for the Spanish Republic, he said, would be alright. He put her at ease. Jim Prendergast told me this story. That brave priest had little enough time for the Irish hierarchy. Bill Gannon told me that he'd once heard O'Flanagan refer to Cardinal Logue derisively as 'That monkey-faced baboon up in Armagh.' (ED)

5. The enemy paid a terrible price also. According to Luis Brolin in his book, *Spain: The Vital Years* whenever Franco read the lists of the dead during the Battle of the Ebro, 'he would lean his head on his clenched fists and occasionally break down.'

   Here's an excerpt from *Spain - A Modern History* by Salvador de Madariaga: '*During the Ebro battle the chaplain of a Navarrese regiment was one evening surprised to observe a "strike" at prayer time when, having in the usual fashion led a prayer "for our dead" no one answered. "What is the matter?" he asked. And a soldier answered: "We want a prayer for our dead and for those of our brothers opposite."'* (ED)

6. In January, 1939, Angela Guest and another nurse threw red paint on the door of number 10, Downing Street, in protest at British foreign policy, a policy that they blamed for the bloodshed in Spain. They were arrested by police after this incident. (ED)

7. In his book, *Writers in Arms* (1967) F. R. Benson referred to Charlie Donnelly as a 'promising English author'! (ED)

8. In addition to the picket at the Somax shirt factory, the Republican Congress also supported protests by small farmers in Achill, County Mayo, striking miners in Castlecomer, County Kilkenny , and workers striking at the De Selby quarries in Bray. (MOH)

9. When Welshman Tom Jones was released from a Spanish prison in 1940, he told us a story in the London office that demonstrated the strength of national feeling amongst people from different countries. Apparently, a group of Germans who were International Brigade members managed to escape from the prison they were being held in. Other Germans who were on Franco's side, or *Nazis*, were based in a small town that was close to this particular prison and they were heard boasting about this successful escape – i.e. that the only Brigade members who'd escaped were the Germans. Englishman Bill Rowe, Secretary of the 'International Brigade Association' was listening to this anecdote at the time and he couldn't understand how national feelings could be so strong as to overrule political and class hatred as between the fascists and the communists. 'We English underestimate the strength of national feeling,' he said. Despite this statement of Bill's, I still think the whole thing was incomprehensible to him. Further examples of this lack of understanding with regard to national pride and feeling on the part of the British was evident in Bill Alexander's book entitled *British Volunteers for Liberty, Spain 1936-1939* and its account of the British Battalion that fought there. A more accurate title for his book would have been *British and Irish Volunteers*…as this was the real national background and make up of that Battalion, particularly in the early stages of the conflict. As relating to the same subject, I received the following letter from the 'International Brigade Association' in London, in June, 1943 requesting contributions.

   It is possible for individuals to send 30s. a week to their friends and relatives in Miranda del Ebro, Spain, through the Red Cross. We ascertained that it is also possible to send remittances covering in advance five weekly payments for the person in question. We have tried everything to send money to Spain as an organisation through the same channel. We failed. The International Red Cross flatly refuses to have anything to do with organisations.

> *We, therefore, enclose £7.10 and should be very grateful if you would forward the sum to the Red Cross to hand it over to Fred Stark, Campo de Miranda del Ebro, Spain. Nationality: stateless (important!) In your application please do not forget to mention that you know the fellow from the Spain days. According to latest information the internees may be moved at any time. It is, therefore, essential that the remittance be made without delay.*

I did as requested. (ED)

10. These documents were held in the archive of the *Irish Labour History Society*. (ED). The collection is now in UCD Archives, Belfield, Dublin (IE UCDA P55). We thank Kate Manning of UCD Archives for her patience and assistance. (BM)

11. In one letter I received from Josefina, she mentioned that she'd heard that her brother Mario Casals was being held in one of the camps in France – Camp de Mesmil-les-Hurlus – thousands of people had fled across the border into France when Franco took control of Catalonia and those who fled were kept in different camps, in conditions that were awful. A few months previously, in June, 1939, I read a letter in the *New Statesman and Nation* from a man named Marcalino Sanchez who'd spent a while in the camp at St. Cyprien. This same camp had been used during the First World War for captured German prisoners. Sanchez had complained to one of the French Army officers about the inhuman conditions in the camp but the officer had replied: 'You Spaniards are a hardy lot. We had the German war prisoners in this camp and they died at the rate of some sixty a day. I cannot understand it. Your death rate is only fifteen a day. Wonderful!' In her letter to me, Josefina had asked whether any of my friends in London could provide any help to her brother. Unfortunately – as I duly discovered – someone could send packages or supplies to the camps themselves but it wasn't possible to contact any individual held in these camps directly. (ED)

Index